MW00713738

MAKING A SPLASH: GRAPHICS THAT FLOW

**GRAPHIC IDENTITIES / PRINT WORK /
ILLUSTRATIONS /
TYPOGRAPHY / ARTEFACTS**

FOR MANY OF US WHO SEEK EXCITEMENT IN ABSTRACTION, IT'S ALL ABOUT STORYTELLING. WE CREATE VISUAL DISRUPTIONS IN ORDER TO SOLVE SUBTLE ERRORS THAT PICK AT OUR BRAINS. WE KEEP IT COMPLICATED, KEEP IT UNREAL. IN PRACTICE, THAT MIGHT MEAN DUMPING PAINT OVER HAND BRUSHWORK OR PILING UP LAYERED NONSENSE IN PHOTOSHOP. BUT THIS IS NOT ABOUT FLAILING AROUND WITH MATERIAL. WE HAVE A CLEAR STORY IN THE BACK OF OUR MINDS. THIS CHAOS IS DIRECTED. WE KNOW WHERE WE'RE HEADED, BUT ALLOW OURSELVES TO GET LOST ON THE WAY. WE WANDER, LETTING INCIDENTS AND ACCIDENTS INFLECT OUR FLOW. IT IS IN THESE MOMENTS OF DISCOVERY, NOT IN THE BLIND PURSUIT OF AN END POINT, THAT THE WORK ACCUMULATES A PARTICULAR ENERGY. THE JOURNEY BECOMES THE DESTINATION. AND THE STORY OF THE JOURNEY IS RECORDED ON ITS SURFACE.

DURING THE LAST FEW YEARS, I HAVE SPENT A LOT OF TIME RESEARCHING ACCIDENTS, USING IMPERFECTION AS A STARTING POINT. MOSTLY IT HAS INVOLVED MAKING A MESS, EXPERIMENTING WITH DIFFERENT MATERIALS AND DOING A LOT OF SECOND-GUESSING. SOMETIMES THE SECOND ACCIDENT MIGHT EVEN BE BETTER THAN THE FIRST. THIS HAS BECOME A BIT OF AN OBSESSION. IT COULD TAKE AN ETERNITY, SINCE I DON'T HAVE A CLUE AS TO WHAT I MIGHT FIND. AN INTERESTING JOB FOR AN IDIOT.

IT'S LIKE MY FRIEND JOSH COCHRAN SAYS, "RIDE THAT TRAIN AS LONG AS IT GOES."

PEOPLE MAKE REQUESTS FOR "SOMETHING I'VE NEVER SEEN BEFORE" — ABUNDANT THINGS, EXPERIMENTAL, DISRUPTIVE, COLOURFUL, ABSTRACT, ICONIC, POP, TACTILE, PAINTERLY, PLAYFUL, SYMBOLIC, HIGH-PERFORMING, LOWBROW, EASY, VIVID, ARTFUL, FASHIONABLE, EXPRESSIVE, GOSSAMER, FLOATING, EXPLOSIVE, LUSCIOUS — THIS LIST IS PROUDLY EATING ITSELF. IN CONVERSATIONS, WE ARE LIKE JAZZED CHATTERBOXES, SPACED OUT AND FREE-ASSOCIATING WHILE STARING AT A LUMINOUS SCREENSAVER.

PSYCHEDELIC IMAGERY WAS ONCE TIED TO STRONG MOVEMENTS: THE SEXUAL REVOLUTION, ENVIRONMENTAL ACTIVISM, POLITICAL AND RELIGIOUS FREEDOM. TODAY, I WONDER WHAT OUR IMAGERY WILL BE REMEMBERED FOR (HOPEFULLY IT'S NOT JUST ABOUT SELLING T-SHIRTS.) MAYBE IT WILL COME TO EMBODY OR REPRESENT A NEW LEVEL OF ACCEPTANCE AND TOLERANCE. MAYBE IT WILL REPRESENT A TIME OF NATURAL DISASTERS, DEPRESSION AND ECONOMICAL CRISIS TROUGH CHAOTIC VIVID IMAGES. MAYBE THIS MOMENT IS FINALLY TRIGGERING US TO TAKE AN ANOTHER DIRECTION. ON THE OTHER HAND, PLENTY OF PEOPLE WHO LOOK AT MY WORK ASK "ARE YOU ON DRUGS?"

I AM WALKING DOWN THE STREET THINKING ABOUT A NEW PIECE FOR AN EXHIBITION. EYEBALLING THINGS IN FRONT OF ME: A DOG PISSING IN THE WIND, TAR SPLATTER ON THE PAVEMENT, A SPRING MATTRESS WIRE FRAME. EASY, LIKE A DOODLE. A CONSTRUCTION SITE HAS A FRESH PLYWOOD WALL BLOCKING THE DRIVEWAY. IT'S A BRILLIANT PATTERN. A CIRCULAR SAW HAS LEFT A HORSE-SIZED HOLE DEEP IN A BUILDING FOUNDATION, REVEALING GRIMY LAYERS OF DIRT. IT'S AN AMAZING CROSS-SECTION. AT MY DESTINATION, THE POLISH GROCERY STORE, THICK JUICE IS SPILLING FROM A HOLE IN THE BOTTOM OF A CARTON. THERE IS NO ONE AROUND ME, SO THIS SIGHT IS A TRUE TREASURE. BY THE END OF THE DAY, THE ONLY THING I CAN THINK OF IS THAT JUICE CASCADE, THE CROSS-SECTION CUT, AND THE DOG PISS. A FEW MORE PIECES TO ADD TO MY MENTAL SLIDE SHOW.

SANTTU MUSTONEN

"THE BATTLE ROYALE BETWEEN THE MODERN AND THE CLASSICAL IS BY FAR MY FAVOURITE MÊLÉE."

MY WORK PRESENTLY EXPLORES THE POWERFUL ALCHEMY OF HARNESSING COLLAGE AND APPROPRIATION ART TECHNIQUES, TO REMIX 'TRADITIONAL' FINE ART PICTURES WITH DYNAMIC COLLISIONS OF FORM AND COLOUR. THIS TECHNIQUE GENERATES TRANSITORY NEW TYPES OF PROVISIONAL IMAGERY THAT POSSESS AN AMALGAM OF THE ENIGMATIC AND THE ACCESSIBLE, OFFERING COMPELLING INTERPLAYS BETWEEN THE RESIDUAL ASSOCIATIONS OF THE ORIGINAL PICTURES AND THE IMPOSED VISUAL COLLISIONS. THIS POWERFUL CREATIVE FLUX DERIVED FROM AN INCREASINGLY COHERENT AND AMPLIFIED HYBRID AESTHETIC, REALLY CONNECTS WITH ME (AND LOOKS EXTREMELY GOOD ON A WALL). MY COMPOSITIONS FEATURED IN THIS BOOK AND MY LATEST IMAGES ON THOMAS-R.COM EXEMPLIFY THIS ACCELERATING DYNAMIC.

MY PRESENT WORK IS A DIRECT CREATIVE REACTION TO MY PROFESSIONAL BACKGROUND AS A TELEVISION GRAPHIC DESIGNER IN WHICH I BECAME INCREASINGLY UNEASY WITH PRODUCING A HIGHLY EDITED AND CURATED VISUAL LANGUAGE. THIS DISCOMFORT LED ME TO START EXPERIMENTING, BRINGING TOGETHER MULTIPLE DIVERSE ELEMENTS TO CREATE IMAGES THAT RE-NEGOTIATE THE NATURE OF COMPOSITION AT MULTIPLE LEVELS IN OUR VISUALLY SATURATED WORLD.

EVERY DAY WE ARE CONSUMERS OF AN INCREASINGLY RAUCOUS VISUAL CULTURE. IT'S A CROWDED, CONSTANTLY MUTATING FIELD OF VISION INCREASINGLY DOMINATED BY THE INTERNET, TELEVISION, ADVERTISING, GAMES, FILMS, SOCIAL MEDIA, ETC. THIS VISUAL MAELSTROM OF OVERLY MEDIATED, REMIXED AND RECONTEXTUALISED IMAGERY, ACTS AS A POWERFUL CATALYST TO FUEL MY EXPERIMENTATION WITH NEW JUXTAPOSITIONS OF FORM AND COLOUR ON OLD GROUNDS. BY APPROPRIATING FINE ART IMAGERY AND FUSING IT WITH 3D RENDERINGS AND PHOTOGRAPHIC SCANS, MY WORK CREATES HYBRID COMPOSITIONS. THAT ATTEMPT TO SUBVERT THE RESTRICTIVE HIERARCHICAL CULTURAL CARAPACES OF HOW SUCH ART PIECES ARE TRADITIONALLY "READ." I CALL IT "COLLISION ART." ALTHOUGH IN A NASCENT STATE, THIS COMPOSITIONAL

EXPERIMENTATION IS BEGINNING TO PRODUCE IMAGES (TO MY EYES) INVESTED WITH INCREASINGLY INTERESTING AND RESONANT AESTHETICS.

MY APPROACH IS PROVOKING A SPECTRUM OF CRITICAL REACTIONS, RANGING FROM "MY FIVE-YEAR-OLD COULD DO THAT," TO "RARE IS IT THAT WE FIND SUCH CONFLICT FOCUSED IN ONE ARTWORK. OFTEN WE SEARCH FOR UNITIES AMIDST THE DISJUNCTURE, HARMONY AMONG DISCORD, BUT THROUGH THE SHEER CONTRADICTION OF THESE IMAGES, ROBSON SETS OUT A GENUINE CHALLENGE TO OUR INTERPRETATIVE SKILLS."

I WORK PRIMARILY IN THE DIGITAL MEDIUM AT PRESENT, AS I NEED TO SUBVERT THE VERY TOOLS I USE AT WORK. ONE BENEFIT IS THAT IT ALLOWS ME TO TAKE ADVANTAGE OF GREATLY ACCELERATED RATES OF VISUAL EXPERIMENTATION, WHICH I USE TO INFORM MY PHYSICAL PAINTING AND DRAWING. MY NEXT STEPS ARE TO INCORPORATE MORE ANALOGUE ELEMENTS TO GENERATE NEW IMPACT WITHIN MY COMPOSITIONS. CREATING HYBRID IMAGES THAT ATTEMPT TO REDRAW THE ESSENTIALLY ARTIFICIAL BOUNDARIES BETWEEN FINE ART AND GRAPHIC DESIGN, WHILST SIMULTANEOUSLY CONFRONTING THE VALUE JUDGMENTS AND SNOBBERY, WHICH CLASSIFIES DIGITAL PRODUCTION AS HIGHLY QUESTIONABLE AND INFERIOR TO 'TRADITIONAL' CRAFT TECHNIQUES.

AS WITH MANY CREATIVE PEOPLE, I ALWAYS HAVE CONFLICTED FEELINGS ABOUT WHAT I PRODUCE. AT HEART MY CORE MOTIVATION REMAINS MY HUNGER TO DISCOVER NEW ITERATIONS OF IMAGE-MAKING, THAT RISE ABOVE THE BACKGROUND VISUAL CACOPHONY OF OUR MEDIA DRIVEN CULTURE.

I ANTICIPATE THAT MY CREATIVE PROCESS IS GOING TO BE QUITE A RIDE, BUT I'M ALREADY TO PRODUCE SOME REALLY EXCITING IMAGES. INVESTED WITH INCREASING VISUAL CLARITY AND AESTHETIC RESONANCES. SO KEEP AN EYE ON THOMAS-R.COM FOR UPDATES AND NEW RELEASES OF PICTURES.

THOMAS ROBSON

THE FLOWING AND INTUITIVE FORCE OF INK IS AN ESSENTIAL QUALITY WE CONTINUOUSLY TRY TO SHOW IN OUR WORK. OUR APPROACH TO DESIGN IS ALWAYS ACCOMPANIED BY ART; IT MIGHT BE NEEDLESS TO SAY BUT CALLIGRAPHY IS A FORM OF ART THAT REMAINS TIMELESS.

EVEN THOUGH IT IS A TRADITION THAT HAS IMMENSE INFLUENCE IN JAPANESE DESIGN, WE INTEND TO FOCUS ON ITS COUNTLESS CONTEMPORARY POSSIBILITIES. THE ERA THAT HAS INFLUENCED ME THE MOST IS THE AZUCHI-MOMOYAMA ERA. ARTISTS LIKE TŌHAKU HASEGAWA FROM THE KANŌ SCHOOL HAVE INSPIRED ME TREMENDOUSLY. AS A DESIGNER, WORKING WORLDWIDE HAS PUSHED ME TO CONFRONT VARIED CHALLENGES, TURNING MY WORK INTO INTERESTING POLYGLOT DESIGN. THE CONSTANT CLASH AND COMPATIBILITY BETWEEN EASTERN AND WESTERN FORMS OF EXPRESSION DEFINE EXACTLY WHO I AM, AND I MAKE A STAND OF THIS FACT THROUGH MY WORK.

BRITISH-BORN WRITER AND PHILOSOPHER ALAN WATTS ONCE SAID THAT ZEN ART IS THE "ART OF THE ARTLESSNESS, THE ART OF THE CONTROLLED ACCIDENT." TO ME, THE COMBINATION BETWEEN GESTURAL AND SPONTANEOUS STROKES WITH THE PRECISION AND THE ACCURACY IN THE USE OF A TYPEFACE AND A GRID SYSTEM IS AN UNCEASING SOURCE OF INSPIRATION. EACH LINE IS MEANINGFUL. THE BEGINNING, THE DIRECTION AND THE ENDING OF LINES ACT TOGETHER TO CREATE A BALANCE BETWEEN ALL THE ELEMENTS INVOLVED. EVEN THE EMPTY SPACE CREATED CAN TESTIFY TO MANY THINGS. BECAUSE THE OUTCOME OF EVERY LINE AND STROKE ARE UNPREDICTABLE, THE DYNAMISM MAKES OUR DESIGN PROCESS MORE INTERESTING. THESE IRREGULARITIES ARE HIGHLY TREASURED AND APPRECIATED, AND CONSISTENTLY SERVED AS THE BASE OF OUR DESIGN.

HOWEVER THE HARMONY AND ELEGANCE OF LINES CREATE NOT ONLY AESTHETIC PLEASURE. THEY ALSO TRANSFER STRENGTH AND DELICACY, EXPRESSIVENESS AND MINIMALISM. ALL OF THESE ADDS NATURAL SPIRIT TO GRAPHICS AND LEAVES THE VIEWER A LASTING IMPRESSION.

OUR PROJECTS ARE OFTEN MONOCHROMATIC, AS BLACK USUALLY TENDS TO BE THE MOST PROMINENT. CONTRAST IS A NOTICEABLE CHARACTERISTIC FROM SOMETHING AS OBVIOUS AS THE USE OF COLOUR TO MORE SUBTLE RESOURCES AS THE USE OF SIZE AND SHAPE. WHEN I CREATE GRAPHICS PARTING FROM INK, I ALWAYS AIM TO EXPRESS IMMATERIAL BUT PROFOUND CONCEPTS SUCH AS FEELINGS AND WIND. I REALISED THAT I, PERSONALLY, COULD ONLY ACHIEVE THIS BY USING INK THIS TECHNIQUE. MR. GEN MIYAMURA, WHO IS AN EXCELLENT JAPANESE CALLIGRAPHER, HAS BEEN MY TRUSTED PARTNER IN CREATION ALL ALONG.

MY UPCOMING EXPLORATION INVOLVING INK IS INSPIRED BY KACHO-FU-GETU, WHICH DENOTES FLOWERS, BIRDS, WIND AND MOON. IN THIS PROJECT I WANT TO KEEP EXPLORING THE JUXTAPOSITION WHEN TRADITION BLENDS IN WITH THE ZEITGEIST.

ARTLESS INC.

CONTENT

BRAND
DYNAMICS

No shapes and stamps make a better trademark than simple yet
characterful flecks and draw the eyes that are constantly on the lookout
for difference, excitement and a warm personal touch.

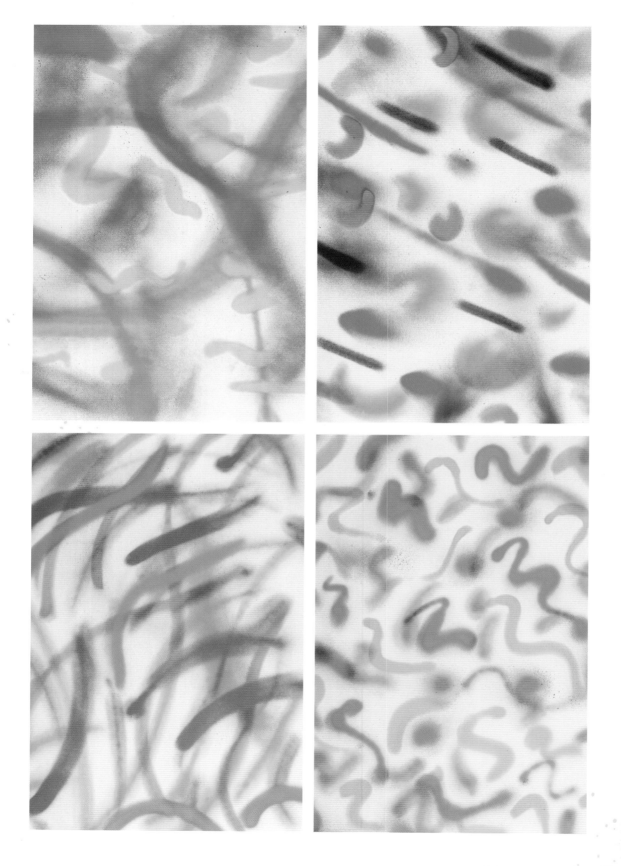

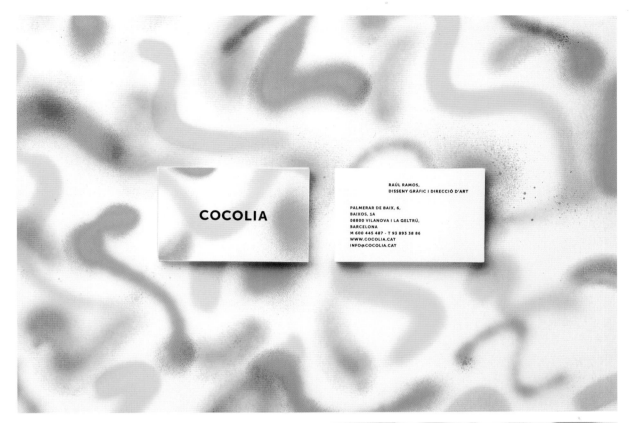

COCOLIA BUSINESS CARD
Cocolia

A low-cost, eccentric identity for design agency Cocolia's own business cards, using random graffiti style prints to reflect the studio's spontaneous and plastic nature. 380g cardboards were manually decorated before cut up and sent off for screenprint, resulting in 600 unparalleled cards.

CHOCOLATE EDITIONS MARBLEISED BAR

Chocolate Editions by Mary & Matt

Mary & Matt pride themselves in crafting
chocolates in small batches by hand. Like its
candy bars, their 2011 special holiday edition
was an artistic surprise. In vibrant reds and blues,
12 eye-popping marbleised wrappers were
handmade to hold the chocolatier's popular
Salted Dark chocolate bar.

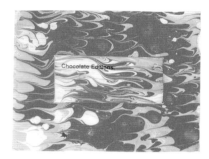

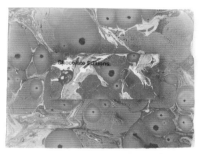

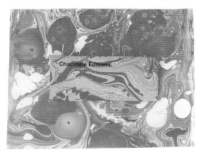

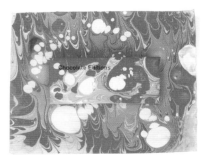

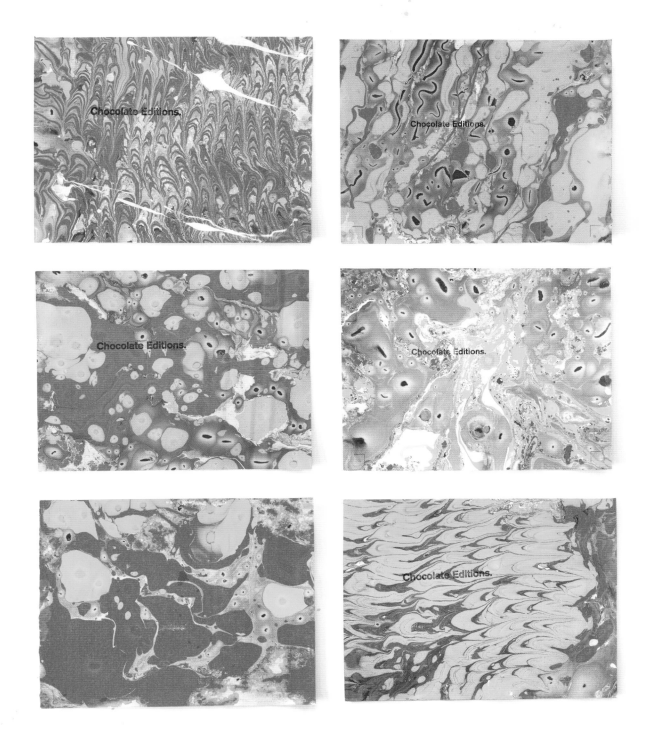

FEMME NATURAL BOOST

Ehrenstråhle & Wågnert

Femme Natural Boost is an all-natural energy drink targeting young women in Stockholm. A no-frills slim packaging with a decent handwriting evoke a sense of confidence and femininity in modern women with a refreshing kick.

Client: Femme Natural Boost

PURE SPRING
Henriette Kruse Jørgensen

A paradoxical packaging
approach to interpret the idea
of "pure" for bottled spring
water. With sprayed types, the
Copenhagen-based designer
takes advantage of glass bottles'
transparency to create an
illusion of ink either dripping
down or diluting in water.

MASTERS RANGE
The Souvenir Society

Organic, abstract shapes and experimental textures in contrasting tones take over the Masters Range, reminding us of how we express ourselves creatively as children. The stationery line contains gift cards, present tags and reusable wrapping clothes to be used as Japanese traditional Furoshiki which the designer duo loves dearly.

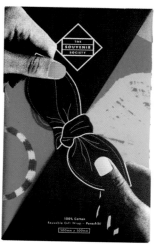

100% Cotton
Reusable Gift Wrap – Furoshiki
500mm x 500mm

ACCIDENT

Austin Young, Brent Leonesio, The Institute for Art and Olfaction (IAO)

An edition of 100 hand-transformed bottles by artist Austin Young are where exotic floral extracts collide with the unexpected notes of gasoline vapour and face powder, an enigmatic fragrance by perfumer Brent Leonesio. A collaborative art piece in support of Young's crowd-sourced art musical, TBD.

Logo & design: Micah Hahn (AutumnSeventy)
Photo: Saskia Wilson-Brown (IAO)

TABLETA POLLOCK

UNELEFANTE

Tableta Pollock is a 54% cocoa chocolate bar named in the famous painter's honour. As a visual connection, eye-catching colour splashes resembling pollock's signature painting style are painted by hand and overlay the entire packaging and candy bar. Each bite is a unique experience rich in colour and flavour.

Chocolatier: Jorge Llanderal
Cacao: Luker Foods
Tea: Leticia Sàenz Tea Sommelier
Photo: Carlos Rodriguez (CAROGA)

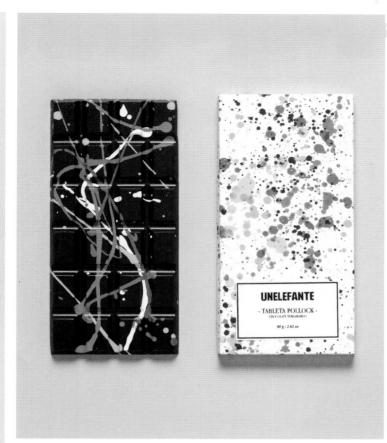

UNELEFANTE

- TABLETA POLLOCK -
(CHOCOLATE SEMIAMARGO)

80 g / 2.82 oz

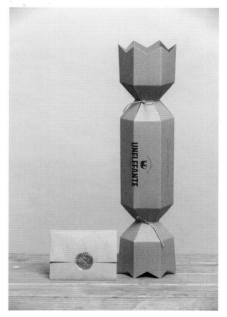

UNELEFANTE

UNELEFANTE

TABLETA POLLOCK

80 g / 2.82 oz

UNELEFANTE

NOVELTY

Anagrama

Novelty is an upmarket boutique that tackles femininity with an edge. Located in the gardened boulevard of Calzada del Valle, the label handpicks curiosities for chic young women. Spontaneous patches of watercolour on their sober peach and black collateral accentuates their classily eccentric style.

Client: Novelty

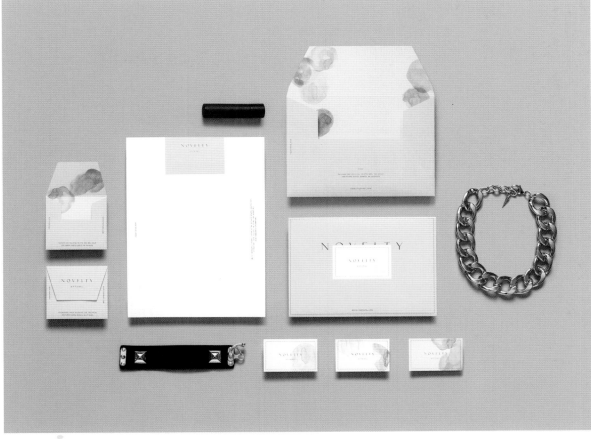

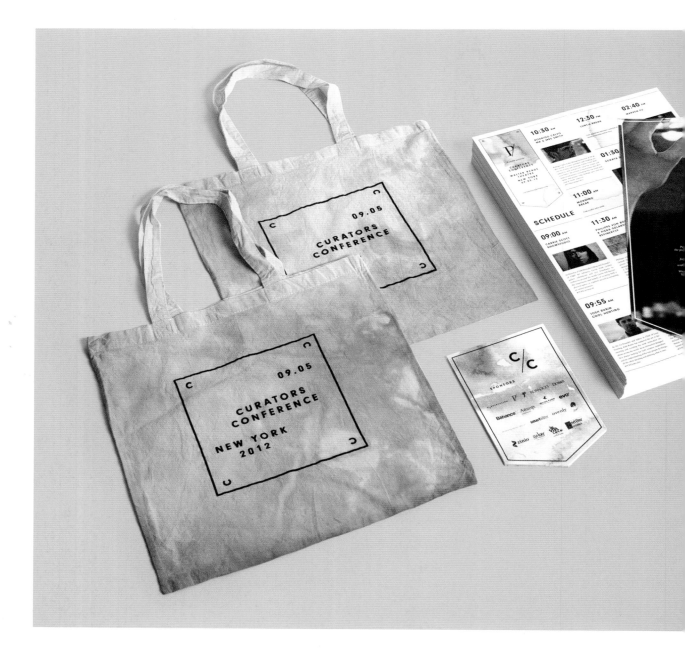

CURATORS CONFERENCE
RoAndCo

Curators Conference was a one-day forum in New York where leading curators convened for discussions around their professional practice. Using watercolour effects, multiple colours bled across the branding elements, evoking contemporary curation's influences on diverse disciplinary.

Client: Portable, The Curators Conference

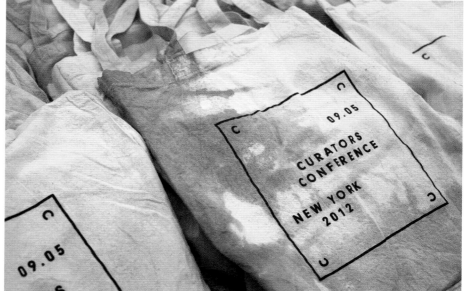

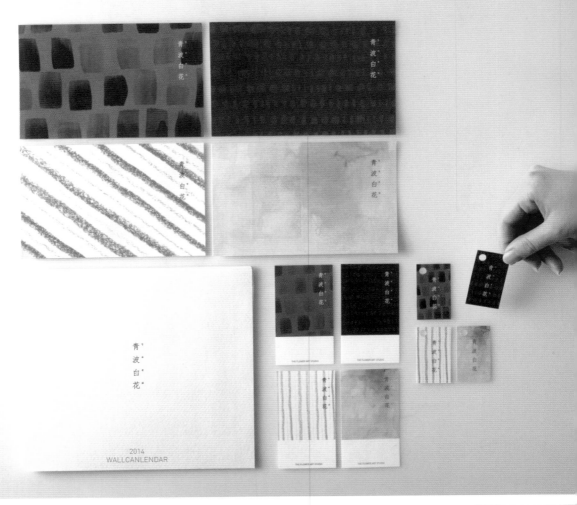

BLUE WAVE,
WHITE FLOWER

daily . j

Graphic identity of a Korean flower art studio is created by hand-painted watercolour and playing tricks with waterproof crayons and candles. Inspired by the country's traditional porcelain, this balmily repetitive duo-colour palette visually sets off the vivacious flowers.

EMINÉ

Maija Rozenfelde

Using the eco-friendly beauty line's
lipstick, eye-shadows as paint, Eminé's
packaging draws attention to the
product's texture in an artistic way.
Translucent layer provides the products
a second skin to convey the product's
colour and forge a graphic interplay
between layers.

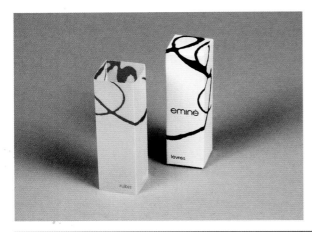

DISH

Taylor Nicholson

Identity for the hibachi restaurant takes artistic reference from Jackson Pollock's unique style of drip painting, which ends around a "dish ring" circling the logotype. Intricacy and intense colours are balanced out by appropriate white space, creating a zesty look to catch the eye.

Special credits: Don Haring (Antoinette Westphal College of Media Arts and Design, Drexel University)

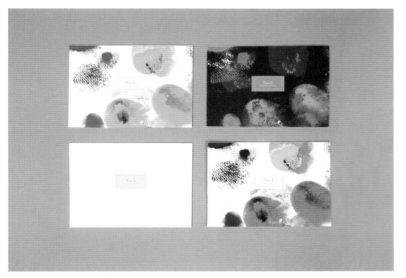

Stiftelsen
Tummeliten

STIFTELSEN TUMMELITEN
Veronika Larsson

A school project commissioned by
Stiftelsen Tummeliten, a foundation
supporting neonatal care in Sweden.
Fingerprints that scatter throughout
the stationery are inspired by the
name of the foundation, which
means "little thumb."

Client: Stiftelsen Tummeliten

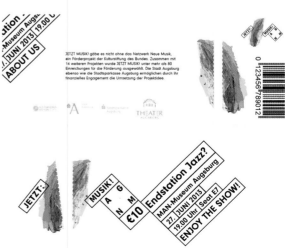

JETZT MUSIK! gäbe es nicht ohne das Netzwerk Neue Musik, ein Förderprojekt der Kulturstiftung des Bundes. Zusammen mit 14 weiteren Projekten wurde JETZT MUSIK! unter mehr als 80 Einreichungen für die Förderung ausgewählt. Die Stadt Augsburg ebenso wie die Stadtsparkasse Augsburg ermöglichen durch ihr finanzielles Engagement die Umsetzung der Projektidee.

JETZT: MUSIK!

John Primmer

Corporate identity redesigned for New Music Society in Augsburg, Germany. Where sounds strike listeners before the lyrics do, acrylic paints figuratively depict experimental music in its most colourful and varied sense and grids serve as "ears" to anchor the brand as a whole. A fluid brand system is meant to fit a diverse lineup.

Client: Augsburger Gesellschaft für Neue Musik
Special credits: Prof. Stefan Bufler (Hochschule Augsburg)

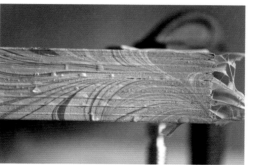

PACT

ACRE

PACT is a destination for people with the common appreciation for honest design goods, tasty foods and forward-thinking hairstyling service. Collaboration of three brands are symbolised by a modified ampersand that spells "PACT," whereas a marbleised visual identity is to depict distinction amidst homogenising brand experience.

Client: PACT

RÉPULSION\ÉMULSION
Morgane Planchenault

French designer Planchenault's final degree project is to explore the art of marbling paper from a scientific perspective. Resulting serene and intricate patterns were produced through repulsion and emulsion that works well on books, reports, communications and notebooks.

JE T'AIME
GRONGAARD Art & Design Studio

Visual identity for a French-inspired bistro in Copenhagen where simple vegetable-based dishes are served in a homely space. To emphasise its unassuming atmosphere, every element in identity system were drawn by hand. The girl's portrait links to the old building, where the bistro located, named after the builder's daughter.

Client: Je t'aime

Je t'aime

HENRIK BREUM
HENRIK@JETAIME.DK
JETAIME.DK
T. 31 15 02 11
CVR. 35514392

Je t'aime

DYBBØLSGADE 9
1721 KØBENHAVN V
T. 31 26 70 69
JETAIME.DK

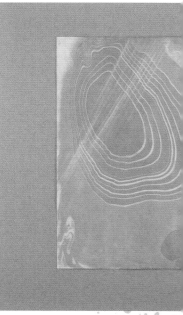

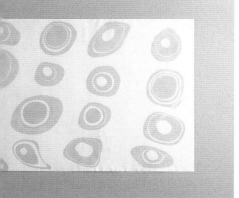

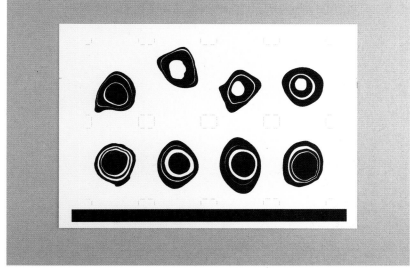

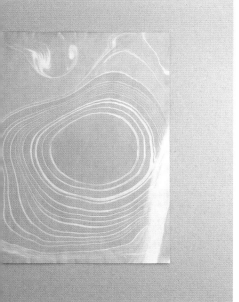

ALMIGHTY
DEMIAN CONRAD DESIGN

Interior and home staging agency Almighty
is looking for a flexible and contemporary
brand system. A solution is found using
the Japanese marbling technique of
Suminagashi. These unique sets of organic
growth rings are paired with industrial
typeface "Gravur" to create contrast.

Photo: Yvain Genevay
Client: Almighty

UNDERWEARABLES SOAP BAR

Spread Studio

Underwearables is a luxurious collection of classic underwear and body care range from Copenhagen. Rooted in the Scandinavian tradition for simplicity and quality, packaging of their soap bars feature key botanical ingredients illustrated in Japanese black ink on plain white wrappings in a clean yet engaging fashion.

Client: Underwearables

CASS ART CARTRIDGE

Pentagram

Packaging design for art supplier Cass Art's own range of cartridge paper pads. Layout, marker, tracing, sketchbooks and so on, pads of various purposes are distinguished on the cover by raw paint marks. A straightforward identification system but not lacking fun.

Photo: Nick Turner
Client: Cass Art

046   047

BY DESIGN OR BY DISASTER

Amin Al Hazwani & Philip Santa

Event identity for an interactive forum that looked into the role of design in constructing a sustainable future. The idea of eliminating creative disciplinary boundaries was translated into a rigid information structure punctuated by wild lettering. Strong colours added impact to command attention for the important topic.

Curation: Prof. Kris Krois, Prof. Alvise Mattozzi
Photo: Tobia De Marco
Newsroom: Nina McNab, Elettra Bisogno
Client: Faculty of Design and Art, Free University of Bozen-Bolzano

KIGO KITCHEN

Clara Mulligan (Creature)

Kigo is a young pan-pacific street food-inspired joint that brings some of the world's most flavourful back alley eats to Boston and Seattle. Dashing brush type that roams their disposable utensils and blunt signage visually recreates the gratifying wok-fire adventure with a touch of American chicness.

Client: KIGO

DESIGNERS BEHIND THE UTS GRAD SHOW

Olivia King & Sebastian Andreassen

A beguiling visual identity for the 2013 University of Technology Sydney graduation show. Inspired by the self-mocking slang of "working one's butts off," the unfortunate cheeks were mischievously depicted by two simple shades throughout the event collateral, a playful creation that needs one to decode.

Collaborators: Nina Harcus, Steph Tsimbourlas
Client: University of Technology Sydney

BOUTIQUE – WHERE ART MEETS FASHION

Tsto

Visual identity for exhibition "Boutique" exploring fashion culture in multiple art forms at Amos Anderson Art Museum. Mediums included music and dance, which the solution captured along with the spirit of collaboration and community. The juxtaposed images were works of participating photographer Juliana Harkki and painter Rauha Mäkilä.

Painting: Rauha Mäkilä
Photo: Juliana Harkki
Client: Amos Anderson Art Museum

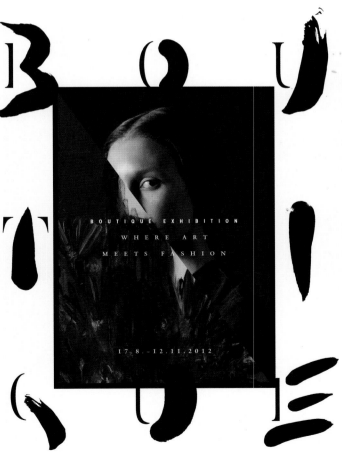

BOUTIQUE EXHIBITION

WHERE ART

MEETS FASHION

17.8.–12.11.2012

PAOLA SUHONEN MIKKO IJÄS KATJA TUKIAINEN SAMU-JUSSI KOSKI TEEMU MUURIMÄKI TERO PUHA SALLA SALIN TIMO RISSANEN MINNA PARIKKA JANI LEINONEN HEIDI LUNABBA TÄRÄHTÄNEET ÄMMÄT ANNA MUSTONEN & CO RAUHA MÄKILÄ JULIANA HARKKI

FÊTE DE LA MUSIQUE 2012

Neo Neo

Event identity for the summer music festival in Geneva, which hosts up to 300 performances in three days. An eclectic approach is set to visualise festival ambiance, with organic forms of mixed colours that suggests integral music styles spanning classical, rock, ethno and hip hop.

Client: City of Geneva

DE TWEE
Twee

De Twee is Dutch for "The Two." Based in Antwerp, Twee is a brother-team whose creative approach combines digital art and handicrafts. The idea "two" guides through their corporate identity from colour scheme through to visual style. Similar yet different, the result says "the two" work perfectly well.

TH-INK
Diego Leyva Caballero

Ink drops make the best element for branding system of the ink and toner company in Mexico City. Key visual was simply created by capturing unforeseen formations of blue ink descending in water, a resplendent brand system by a medium closely related to the brand.

Client: TH·INK Toner Solutions

LIME
ONY

Brand identity for LIME, a café that offers Japanese and European cuisine in Moscow. A blob of fresh green aquarelle stain sums up the eatery's advocacy of simple living, and evolves to suggest what attribute to such lifestyle on packaging and across its stationery items.

NAIVE

Agnes Herr, Gita Elek

Inspired by a strange dream, Naive is a fictitious visual identity for a cultural centre for young people. Stencilled logo with dripping paint in mint colours adds energy and spirit to the system. The pair also wishes to symbolise the obscure state of being in and out of dreams with liquid flowing down animal figures.

ART
WWW.NAIVE.COM
WWW.NAIVE.COM
• SURPRISE EXHIBITIONS •
EVERY WEEK
Next exhibition starts at 11th January 2014.
You can buy the tickets on our website · www.naive.com/tickets · or in the NAIVE club
NAIVE
666
UNICORN STREET
CANDYLAND

· SURPRISE WORKSHOPS ·
EVERY WEEK
Next workshop starts at 11th January 2014.

NAIVE
UNICORN STREET   CANDYLAND

· CAFE, PUB, RESTAURANT ·
EVERY WEEK
Our cafe, pub and restaurant is nonstop.

NAIVE
UNICORN STREET   CANDYLAND

· SURPRISE CONCERTS ·
EVERY WEEK
Next concert starts at 11th January 2014.

NAIVE
UNICORN STREET   CANDYLAND

· DANCE AND NIGHT CLUB ·
EVERY WEEK
Next dance party starts at 1th January 2014.

NAIVE
UNICORN STREET   CANDYLAND

MIKSER FESTIVAL 2012

Lorem Ipsum Studio

Visual identity for Mikser Festival, a major
creative arts festival in Belgrade, Serbia. As
the brand system's core element, improvised
lettering and images created varied distortions
to underline the event's dynamism and the
new programme structure — a major change
for the 2012 edition.

Collaborator: Bratislav Milenkovic
Photo: Milica Mrvić
Client: Mikser Festival

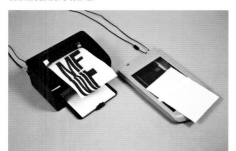

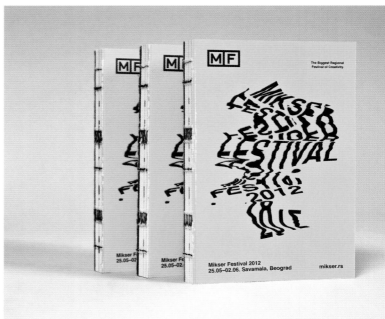

ORGANIZATOR
PRODUKCJA

ARTYSTA

XXII FESTIWAL ARS CAMERALIS

Marta Gawin

Taking painter Michał Minor's handwriting as the motif, the raw, distinctive strokes on visual identity unfold the annual art festival's central theme, "I know what others do not know." Old gold and black reinforced a quest for truth, with elaborated themes corresponding to the four featured disciplines — music, film, art and literature.

Brush lettering: Michał Minor
Photo: Barbara Kubska
Client: Ars Cameralis Silesiae Superioris

PRINTED
TEMPTATION

FREITAG
20.9.13

23:00 UHR
KAUFLEUTEN

Be it a key visual element or an ornamental backdrop, a drip-splash
mark or a little colour wash can always capture viewers' imagination
and keep their eyes on the poster or mailer for a longer while.
Handwork will quell artistic yen.

DJS:
STYLEWARZ (D)
CERTIFIED
GRO

HIP HOP
CLASSICS
TRAP

Mistletone presents

The Clean

Wed 9 March	Thu 10 March	Fri 11 March	Sat 12 March
Factory Theatre	The Zoo	The Corner	Golden Plains
Sydney	Brisbane	Melbourne	

mistletone.net

THE CLEAN

Alex Fregon

Gig poster for The Clean, a kiwi guitar-pop royalty, promoting the band's first Australian tour since 1989. Easily passes for a kid's drawings, this lighthearted depiction matches well with the band's history of hand-drawn, hypnagogic album art.

Client: Mistletone Records

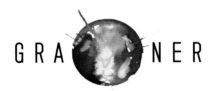

GRANER 2011

Cocolia

As part of Barcelona City Council's Art Factories programme, Graner is a multifunctional dance centre providing artists a space to choreograph, reside and to draw dance closer to the public. Colour-infused globes in this winning brand identity proposal suggest a blast of imagination, experimental and dynamic nature of the art form.

Client: Graner

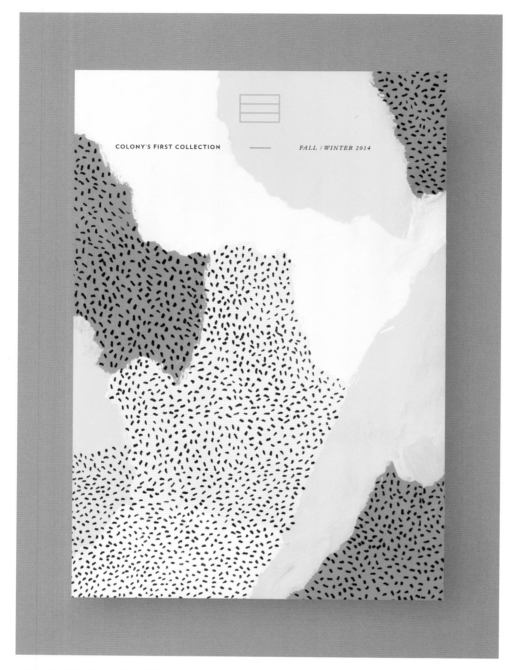

COLONY'S FIRST COLLECTION ——— *FALL / WINTER 2014*

COLONY FOOTWEAR POSTER

Jules Tardy

Prelaunch brand campaign for Colony, a quality footwear collection for men. By publishing graphic posters and pictures, the campaign defines modern man and establishes connections with Ethiopia's high land where the brand sources leather for shoe-making.

Client: Colony Footwear

S-GROUP GIFT CARDS

Leo Karhunen

Collaborating with illustrator Stina Persson, a set of four gift cards is designed for a Finnish retailing cooperative, S-Group. Loose, ethereal illustrations drawn from nature extends beyond the cards onto packaging, making the set an elegant collectible on top of utility.

Creative direction: Erkki Izarra
Illustration: Stina Persson
Photo: Irina Hurme
Client: S-Group
Special credits: 358

SONGS UNDER COVER

Bratislav Milenkovic

An album curated by POP Depression, its cover art consists layers of spontaneous shapes and doodles, depicting diverse musical styles of the 12 selected local bands to each cover one song by visiting artists who played on the Belgradian radio show´s concerts in the past decade.

Client: POP Depression

19

Lisse Moro Rolbaun Marion Braun Cross-
pattern Annual Report Comeback King
Chasa Redax-Voux Holland Scrambled Egg
Softly Waterstadt Babylove Una Vita Japan
Cyan Transtomador till Monde Flottant
ifio Melbourne Continental Hybridity
Geofgrund Cooling Doppelkopf Adia Abeba
Coffree & Bach Hero La Rouge El La Noir
Caracas Passavant Nelson Black Fungus Alp
Signatur Speed Limit Japan Alp Automatic
Strada del Sol Mondia Mere Fine Arts
Bel Ami Tokyo Knauf Substitute Meer Cut
Die Red Air Sgofsatz Transtomador 14.6
Fry Rosemarie Les Fleure Du Mal Posse Aux
Lions Lisse Perfect Pigeon No Return
Speed Limit Revolution Negresco Flashlight
Singen En Route Suze Explosion Sky
Oakwood Rico

FIRST CUTS –
HARALD F. MÜLLER

büro uebele visuelle kommunikation

A printed elucidation of artist Harald F. Müller's work
at the interior of Zurich's Prime Tower in Switzerland.
With words flipped and tilted in a hidden order, this
seemingly absurd text arrangement is also a reflection
of Müller's unique take on typeface design. Bold
strokes complete the idea with a tint of colour.

Publishing: Lars Müller Publishers
Text & editing: Gerd Blum, Johan F. Hartle, Mike Guyer
Client: Harald F. Müller

100

Above all it is important to point
out that we can only maintain our
prosperity in Europe if we belong
to the most innovative regions in
the world.
Angela Merkel

0 123456 789012

One Hundred Euro

100

One Hundred Euro

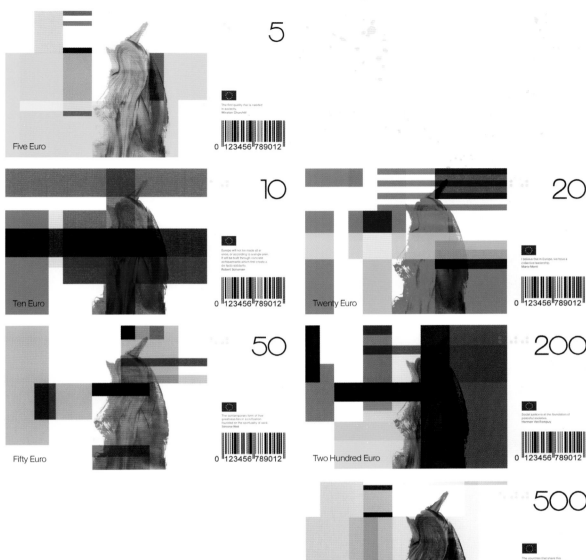

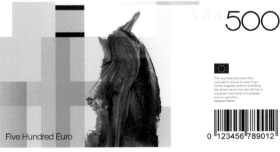

EURO BANKNOTES RETHINK

Coast

It is Coast's turn to give a daily object a makeover in ICON Magazine's Rethink feature, in which they proposed a redesign of Euro banknotes. Spiced up by freeform watermarks and a colourful modular composition of EU member state flags, the notes are envisioned to be printed on enduring polypropylene.

Client: Icon Magazine

Another Planet Entertainment presents

THE NATIONAL
with Local Natives
& Wye Oak

December 3, 2011

Bill Graham Civic Auditorium, *San Francisco, California*

© AnotherPlanetEntertainment.com · No. 26 · Artwork by Sans Pareinus

THE NATIONAL GIG POSTER

There Is

Gig poster for Brooklyn band
The National's live show in San
Francisco. The key visual is a mixed
media photorealistic butterfly that
melts in dripping paint.

WILDLIFE
studio hausherr

First flyer for ongoing party series, Wildlife, organised by club Kaufleuten in Zürich, Switzerland.

Logo: Sascha Bente
Concept & photo: Tobias Faisst

THE BRIDGE BETWEEN LIFE & DEATH

Non-Format

CD packaging and poster for Bristol-based musician Zoon Van Snook's album. Fluid cover art matches well with a modified chisel-serif version of Non-Format's custom typeface City Modern especially for the booklet and poster.

Illustration: Halldór Ragnarsson, Árni Þór Árnason
Client: Lo Recordings

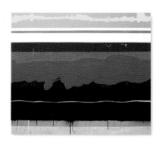

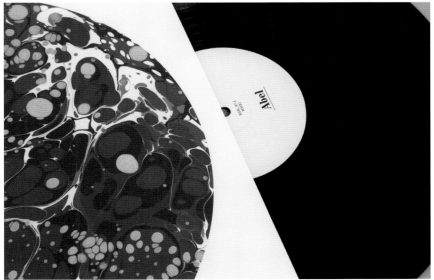

NON, N°.1
David McFarline

Vinyl cover design for UK-based music Noncollective's own first limited edition EP "NON, N°.1." Inspired by the Aegean Sea, cover art is created by marbling with blue and white paints to illustrate swelling waves and exquisite oceanic charisma.

Client: Noncollective

AUFGETAUCHT

Astrid Doerig

Waters of Lake Constance has inspired the opening invitation and give-away's design of Atelier im Sandkasten, a maker space for like-minded DIY enthusiasts. Themed "Auftauchen – ascending," it is metaphoric of how ideas emerge in this Goldach-based workshop sharing the lake view.

Client: Atelier im Sandkasten

Seewies-
strasse 1
9403
Goldach
(Parkplätze vorhanden)

Mit ÖV erreichbar von:
Bahnhof Horn
Bahnhof Rorschach (Hafen)
Bahnhof Rorschach
Bushaltestelle Rietli
▶ zu Fuss

27.10.12

Vir
hen
uf

öffnet die Tore
und stellt aus

27.10.12

Vir
chen
uf

öffnet die Tore
und stellt aus

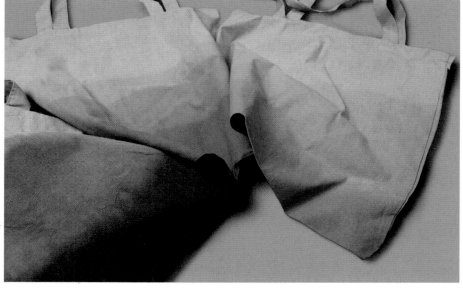

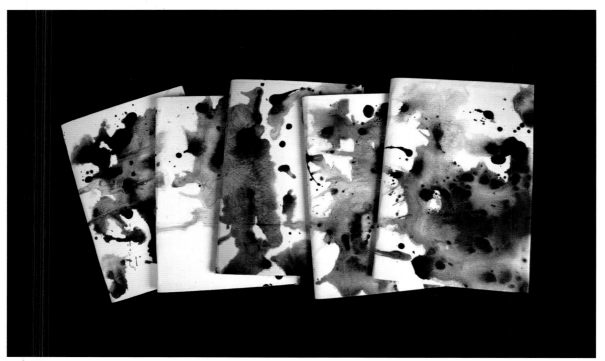

SIX MEMOS

Adrian Newman

Set of six sketchbooks created as an
artistic response to Six Memos for the
Next Millennium, elaborated notes on
what to be cherished in literature, written
by Italo Calvino. Produced as a school
project, Newman uses American poet
Emily Dickinson's words to denote the
similarities between literature and design.

*Special credits: Kelly Monico (Metropolitan
State University of Denver)*

SOUND:

artless Inc.

Nut pine, chrysanthemum and balloons, some distorted, some animated by splashes of ink, these delicate freeze panes are representative of music compilation in "sound:" volume 1-4, post-classical healing sounds composed by sound-maker Leo Sato and Chikao Maruyama.

Client: artless records

noiselessly
by leo sato

artwork by
shun kawakami(artless)

caligraphy by
gen miyamura

flower by
nobuaki kawahara (ren)

sound*
3

noiselessly
by chikao maruyama

artwork by
shun kawakami(artless)

caligraphy by
gen miyamura

balloon art by
daisy balloon

sound*
2

noiselessly

artwork by
shun kawakami(artless)

caligraphy by
gen miyamura

sound*
1

noiselessly
by leo sato

artwork by
shun kawakami(artless)

caligraphy by
gen miyamura

flower by
nobuaki kawahara (ren)

sound*
4

ISETAN NEW YEAR DISPLAY

artless Inc.

Display design at the time-honoured Japanese department store during 2011 new year. Bokusu calligraphy fused momentum with imagery of longevity and good fortune and exploited the play of light and shadows at their Shinjuku branch.

Client: ISETAN

AMORE + FÖLLINGE
Amore

Design agency Amore celebrates the start of fall by treating clients with organic goodness from Swedish skincare label Föllinge. Refurnished in black and white, the gift bundles are encased in paper cylinders dashed with a single ink stroke, a robust declaration of how simple and clean wellness can be.

Client: Amore + Föllinge

BARN OWL

El Señor Gómez & Srta. Swallow

Promotional poster for the San Francisco-based drone metal duo's 2012 Europe tour stood out in minimalistic aethetics. The infinite ghostly void yielded from the experimental meld of olive oil, salt and black oil paint visualises the band's dark music.

Client: Barn Owl

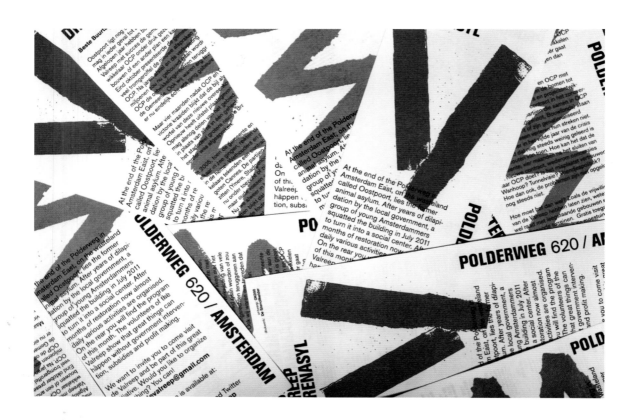

VALREEP PROGRAMME

OK200

Monthly programme poster for "De Valreep," a squatting cultural venue in Amsterdam. Stressing De Valreep's DIY mentality, OK200 added an illustration layer with natural forms to the background and produced the screenprints by hand. The flyers were riso-prints made by "De Stencilkelder."

Client: Op de Valreep

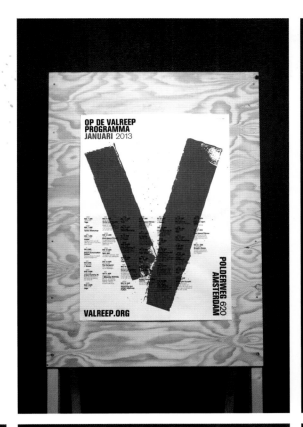

MODALISBOA FREEDOM INVITATIONS

thisislove design studio

Held every March and October, LisboaFashionWeek is a major happening in the Portuguese design scene. Dynamic burst of clashing colours roam an array of show invitations at its 38th winter edition and set off respective designer names, bringing out the theme of "Freedom."

Client: ASSOCIAÇÃO MODALISBOA

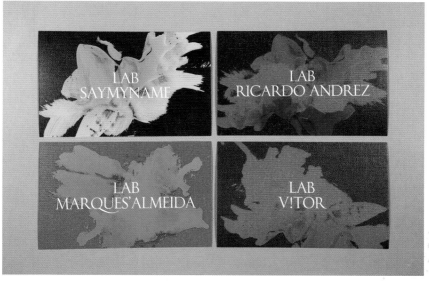

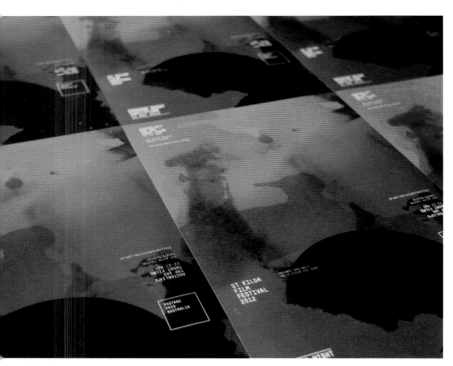

ST KILDA FILM FESTIVAL 2012
Studio Brave

Visual identity for the 2012 edition of Australia's leading short film festival celebrates film maker's vision and imagination. Erratic haze of colours are framed up by abstract geometric shapes, forging a kaleidoscopic campaign system.

Client: City of Port Phillip

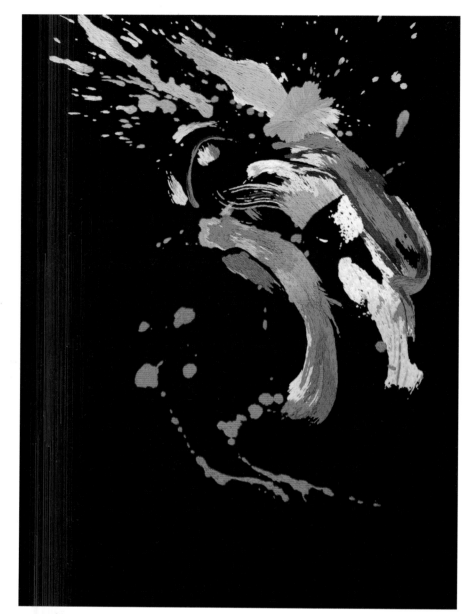

HFTAB EXHIBITION
Maricor/Maricar

Realised with needle and stitches, the designer-duo grasped form of flying paint released from a burst balloon at a millisecond. The embroidery piece was developed for an exhibition initiated by Handsome Frank in 2012, in which artists created art in response to twitter followers' suggestions.

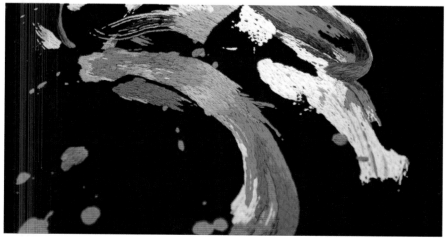

BLANCLAB 2012

Cocolia

Blanclab is an initiative of Blanc. Festival, a one-day lecture marathon held in the city of Vilanova i la Geltrú on technology applied to graphic design in video-games, web design, programming and animation. Set of four posters visualise both complementary disciplines with pictograms and brush strokes.

Client: Blanclab

UNCOMFORTABLE TRUTHS

NB, Akio Morishima

V&A invited 11 contemporary artists to stage installations in light of the bicentenary of the parliamentary abolition of transatlantic slave trade. The exhibition's identity is connected by a rainbow of ink drops and lines, which became silhouettes of participating artists and on-site graphic trails.

Client: V&A

BONDO

Rikako Nagashima

Retail store BONDO prioritises craftsmanship in the art and crafts they stock. Their visual identity is extended to suggest happiness derived from the connections between individuals and that between humans and the world. Vintage imagery and the glue are a nod to handwork and the past when daily necessities were largely made by hand.

JEANASiS

DRAWING MYSELF

JEANASIS
Rikako Nagashima

The 2011 fall campaign for urban wear brand documented how JEANASIS girls played with brush and ink. Themed "Drawing Myself," a poster catalogued the collection on one side and a spirited ink painting on the other. The folded poster was strung and distributed with a Polaroid picture and a tag.

MERCEDES-BENZ FASHION WEEK TOKYO 2014/15

Rikako Nagashima

Like fashion, these organic shapes and lines engender the person they surround. Everyone holds the power to draw and define who they are just as they dress themselves. "Draw your life" concludes the message that Fashion Week TOKYO 2014 Fall/Winter wishes to bring.

AIC – RE-NEUE

Derek Kim

A poster series for the last show at the private exhibit space of Altamira Industrial Complex (AIC) before it closes for renovation. Key visuals are to remind viewers that the space is under construction, with sprays of bright colours to denote the excitement of future exhibitions.

Client: AIC

Re—Neue

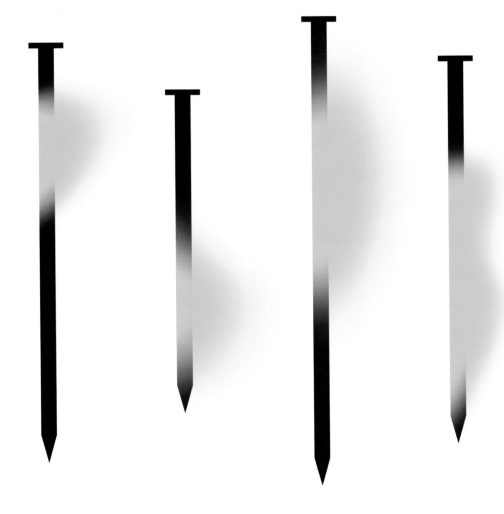

We are moving to a new space, hoping to provide our loyal supporters with a better environment for our artistic community to thrive in. Due to the uncertain nature of this process, our current space will be closed until further notice.

We would like to invite you to our last event, celebrating 5+ years of commitment to the development of art, music and design.

Your continued support has allowed the AIC to provide artists with an open space for creativity and freedom of expression at no cost. We truly value your membership and will do our best to maintain a high level of commitment for AIC's artistic community.

Thank you.

at the Altamira Industrial Complex (South Annex)

Friday July 26th, 2013 6:00pm - 9:30pm

Event's date and time are subject to change

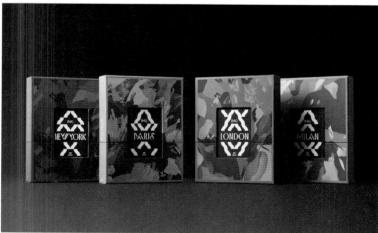

IMG MODELS
SHOWCASE S/S14

Anti

A floral motif with endless variations accent the
natural beauty that distinguishes IMG models
in the industry. To contrast the wild, unruly
beauty of flowers, a more formal yet illustrative
typeface was conceived based on the golden
ratio. Four colour schemes set apart the
departments in New York City, Paris, London
and Milan.

Client: IMG Models

SVA MAGAZINE #6
Anti

At the time SVA commissioned Anti to work up the editorial design for its sixth issue, the team was experimenting with the interactions and viscosity of various paints. The result was a range of intricate shapes and ornamental patterns rendered by mixing and smudging colours to juxtapose the beauty and grotesque in human sexuality.

Photo: Baard Lunde, Henrik Bulow, Svein Bringsdal, Fabrizio Rainone, Johanna Nyholm
Client: SVA Magazine

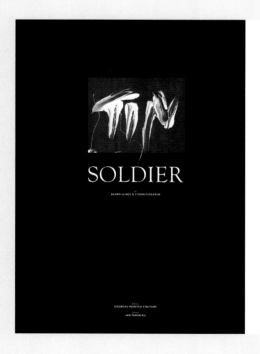

THE

SIX STAR

GIRL

By
JOHANNA NYHOLM & ISABELLE HAWI

Dress
CARIN WESTER

Sunglasses
MINIMARKET

Necklace
VIVEKA BERGSTRÖM

Bracelet
VIVEKA BERGSTRÖM

Earrings
CORNELIA

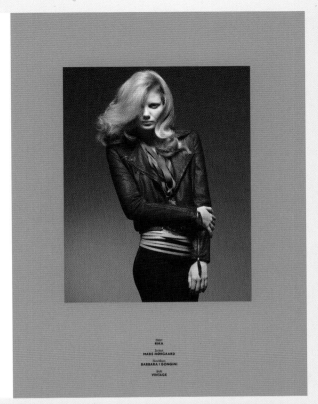

Shirt
RIKA

Jacket
MADS NØRGAARD

Necklace
BARBARA I GONGINI

Belt
VINTAGE

ALPHA

MALE

By
HENRIK BÜLOW & ALEXANDRA CARL

Hat
DAVID ANDERSEN

Headpiece
KOPENHAGEN FUR

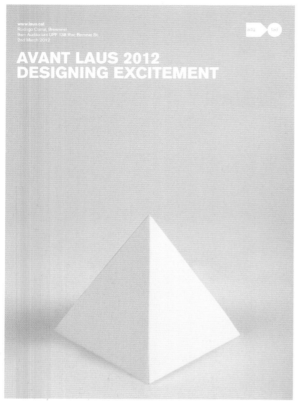

**AVANT LAUS 2012
DESIGNING EXCITEMENT**

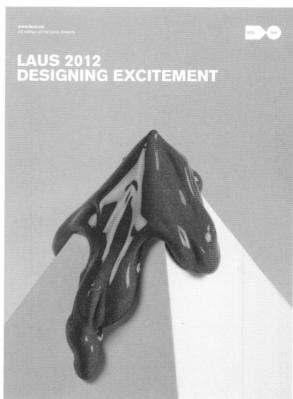

**LAUS 2012
DESIGNING EXCITEMENT**

**LAUS NIGHT 2012
DESIGNING EXCITEMENT**

LAUS AWARDS 2012

Dharani Bassols & Montse Galbany

A communication campaign for the acclaimed Laus Awards hosted by ADG-FAD. Centring on the idea of orgasm as a metaphor for career success, the project featured a sensual visual image where fulfilment figuratively flows over the pleasure.

Concept: Oscar Torres
Client: Laus Awards (ADG-FAD)
*Special credits: Michel Goday, Elisava
School of Design & Engineering*

MUD 2012
SOPA GRAPHICS

Poster design for the Spanish folk music festival in Lleida gives conventional impression on this genre a refreshing twist, just what MUD does by introducing neo-folk to audience. Dripping bird symbolises transformation, hinting music at the festival is evolving into a new music style.

Photo: Joan Cantó
Client: Guerssen Records

2013 JTBC TOMORROW CONFERENCE
studio fnt

South Korea's national cable TV network and broadcaster JTBC hosts Tomorrow Conference annually and internally to formulate future plans. As key visuals, revolving around the broadcaster's initial, abstract forms visually express the company's potential and possibilities.

Client: JTBC

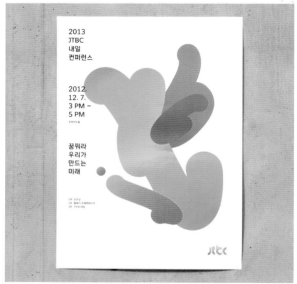

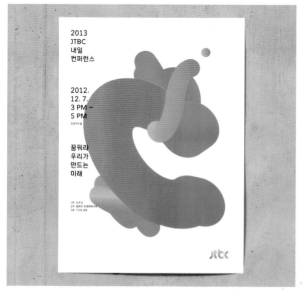

FLOW FESTIVAL 2013

Tsto

The identity for the music and arts festival united the urban tribe with a metaphorical mantra of visual wordplay. Along with Santtu Mustonen's illustrations, the recurring letters and images form the system's whole. "Emotions" was the core of Flow Festival 2013 and was communicated through colours, illustrations and type treatment.

Illustration: Santtu Mustonen
Client: Flow Festival

OVERPOWERED REMASTERED
Spiros Halaris Studio

A personal project that re-envisages covers for Irish singer-songwriter Róisín Murphy's second album, "Overpowered." Closing up on images of a psychedelic mixture of thick paint and its protruding veins of pigment add volume to the design.

TYPOGRAPHY
Spiros Halaris Studio

A personal project experimenting type treatment with various mediums and techniques.

RETHINK DANCE
Ghost Design

Constantly evolving and on the move, Rethink Dance is an art driven forum where choreographers and dancers exchange inspirations. The moves and energy were metaphorically marked with rough brushes on large canvases and photographed to create prints. Project covers posters, leaflets and bags.

Illustration: Anders Emil Sommerfeldt

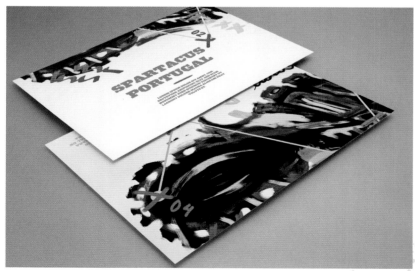

SPARTACUS

Apex Studio

Using running shoe as an universal symbol, a zestful type captured Spartacus' violent nature and the physical endurance required to complete the obstacle race. The illustration layer also adds intensity that prevails the game.

Client: Amigos do Trail

WEDDING INVITE

Studio Band

Taking inspirations from
Rorschach inkblot test drawings,
the abstract imagery of dried
flowers and oil on water
illustrated the uniqueness of
love and its varied meanings
to individuals. Invitations were
printed on textured uncoated
stocks and produced as A5
booklets with gold foiled names
and hand stitching.

EUROPEAN DESIGN AWARDS 2012 CATALOGUE

Designers United

Art direction and design for European Design Awards 2012 catalogue, revealing the core of Awards' logo on the front cover as its coating melts, and leaving dabs of the black substance at the back. The 2012 Awards ceremony was hosted in Helskinki, Finland.

Client: European Design Awards

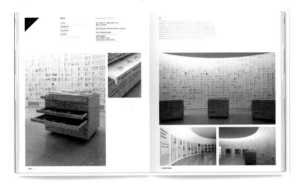

BRONZE

SIGNS & DISPLAYS

31

TITLE
Aufbau Haus
COMPANY
Markdorra GmbH
COUNTRY
Germany
CLIENT
Moritzplatz 1
Entwicklungsgesellschaft GmbH

DESIGNERS
Sibylle Schlaich, Anne von Borries
Bastian Rennen, Christian Witt
CREATIVE DIRECTORS
Heike Nehl

FSB
GALERIE EDITION BRAUS
MINIMUM EINRICHTEN
NEUMANN & RODTMANN
QUITOBERLIN
STADTTERRASSE

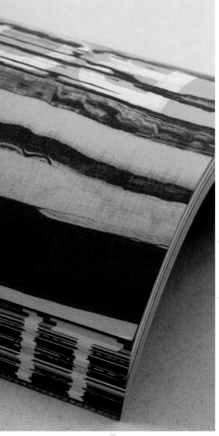

MAZINE BRAND BOOK
Stahl R

Brand book to provide insight into the various activities and people of Mazine, a clothing brand based in Ruhrgebiet, the largest industrial area in Germany. Six unique covers represent the six uniquely designed chapters of the book.

Creative direction: René Natzel

VISUAL
IMPACT

Take a close look at that splash and contemplate the details
before it falls on your face. New technology has enabled image-makers
to hold time, enhance accuracy and fabricate a dream world for curious
eyes to immerse in. Visual revolution proposes a new artistic statement
in the new era.

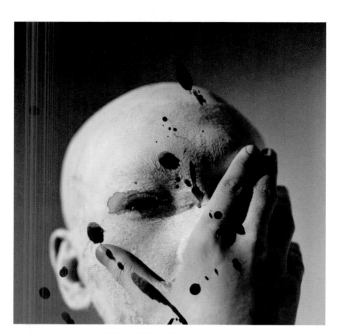

PARADOXICALLY, YOURS
SILLY THING

Album sleeve cover art juxtaposing imagery and drawings to illustrate the artist, Juno Mak's creative world. Colour and monochrome portraits together rendered the conflicts and sinful desire living in the demonic monk.

Photo & painting: Nobuyoshi Araki

FATE(S)
TYMOTE

Album sleeves design for Gummy's
mini album, Fate(s). Colours, patches
and basic geometries conjure up the
Korean artist's music world where
whimsical thoughts clash with reality.

Art Direction: Mitsuishi Naokazu
Photo: Hashimoto Hideyuki
Client: Avex Group

GUMMY
FATE(S)

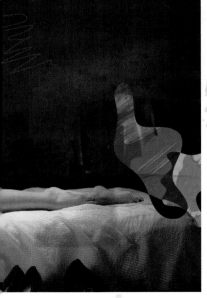

HINT MAGAZINE: GASLIGHT

Sans Colour

Art direction and design for an interactive editorial for online Hint Magazine to coincide with Paris fashion week. A surreal universe was built on the theme of Gaslight, where viewers could "travel" and close in on the models and their clothing. The project was realised at Bleed, with motion and music by Bjørn Gunnar Staal.

Production & Sound:
Bjørn Gunnar Staal
Client: Hint Magazine

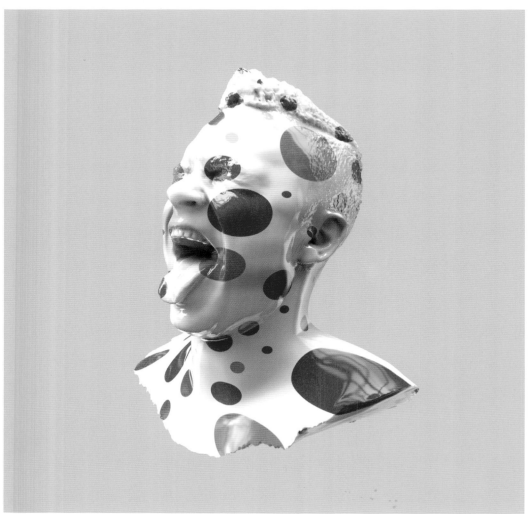

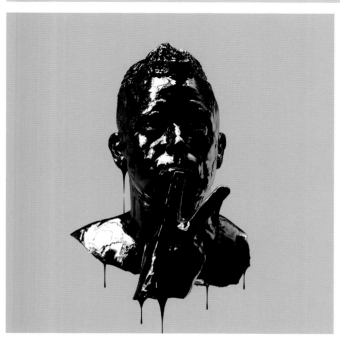

TAKE THE CROWN
Tom Hingston Studio

Album campaign for British singer
Robbie Williams's album Take the
Crown. Harnessing 3D and 4D
scan, both movements and static
expressions of the artist are captured
and rendered with dramatic patterns
and dripping inks as animations for
both screens and live shows.

*3D rendering: Oliver Fawcett
Client: Farrell Music*

145

TRANSFER

Kevin Corrado

Is ocean a paint reservoir or blue by nature? Depicting hands soaked in paints as if they were picking colours from the landscapes, Transfer speaks about the intense connections between the natural environment, and the colours we project on to it.

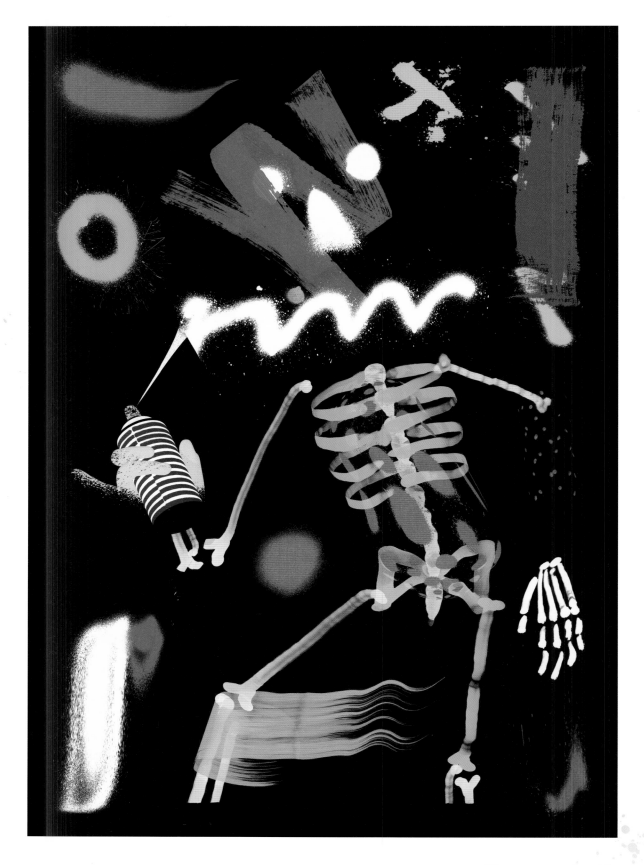

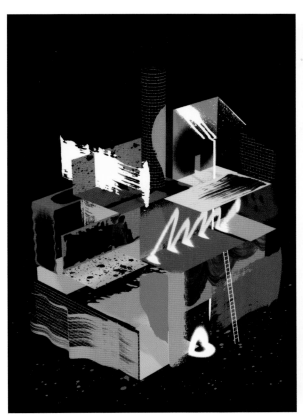

SANTTU MUSTONEN COLLECTIONS

Santtu Mustonen

A peculiar mix of strokes, forms, colours and volumes playfully interprets "Writing My Name," "Hall of Fame," and "Spaghetti," from left to right. The digital prints were produced for a group exhibition held at Make Your Mark Gallery in Helsinki.

COLLISION ART

Thomas Robson

Collision Art is an artistic
experiment on form and colour.
Aiming to seek resonance in
the media driven visual culture
of modern society, artist
Thomas Robson defaces solemn
characters on classic portraits
with dashing paint, either in the
form of pigment or digital 3D
graphics.

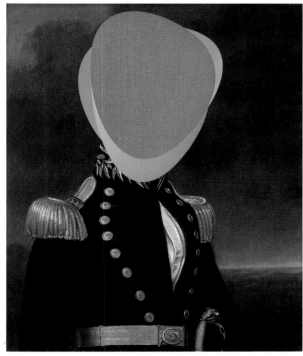

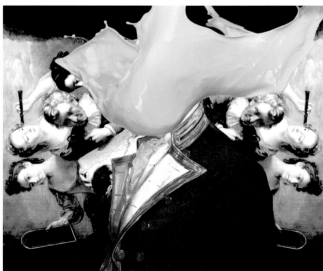

FLUID WHITE

Thomas Robson

Collision Art by Thomas Robson using various states of white pigment or digital art that smudge the subjects in the oil painting portraits. Juxtaposition between fine art and modern digital art is reflective of our fast-moving and remixed cultures.

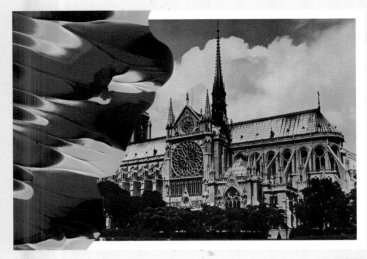

SOUVENIRS DE PARIS

Leslie David

Fascinating paint textures and colours together fashion a new term for French romance. Slightly pressed, the thick paints yielded a variety of patterns and gradations in stark contrast to the classic Parisian monuments. The imagery was produced into eight postcards commissioned by concept store colette.

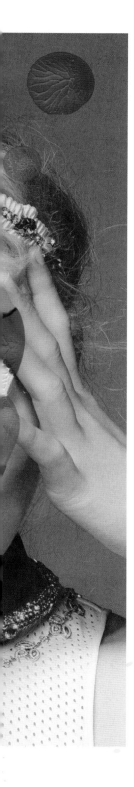

PAINTING PLEASE!

Leslie David

Illustrations created to celebrate PLEASE! Magazine's 5th birthday. Twelve artists and designers were given complete freedom to regenerate archive images of the magazine. Textured paint was Leslie David's approach, breathing new energy and colours into editorials of The Little Princess Issue.

Photo: Nagi Sakai

1

2

3

4

ART INTERVENTION
Ernesto Artillo

A collection of illustrations reconstructing human faces with colours and paint. Samples of such art intervention include collage artwork for Glamour Italia and Bulgari (1), campaign for Six Lee (2), and artwork for IMG Models Worldwide (3-5).

Modelling: Amanda Murphy, Kenley, Zen Sevastyanova
Photo: Willy Vanderperre, Terry Gates

SIX LEE 2014

Ernesto Artillo

2014 Collection campaign for Six Lee, a
menswear-fashion brand with bases in
Antwerp and Hong Kong. Collages made
with pictures by Zeb Daemen and Artillo
himself beautifully captured the collections'
dreamy details alongside artworks fusing
photography and painting.

Photo: Zeb Daemen

STROKES
Tomas Markevičius

An graphic experiment, interpreting fashion shots with digital paintbrush comparable to real paint. Bright and bold colour background boosts classic yet contemporary-looking fashion imagery.

Photo: Marton Perlaki, Tsatsani Katarina, Justin Borbely, Matthew Josephs, Ahn Joo Young

{ photo by }
SARA PELLEGRINO

{ model }
KORLAN MADI @leon

{ make-up }
SOFIA ÁLVAREZ CARREÑO

{ special thanks }
LEAM LUXURY STORE

OVER

Sara Pellegrino

A series of high fashion photography for independent magazine Sicky's exclusive editorial. Photographer Sara Pellegrino adds artistic touch to designer clothes by freestyle splatters and strokes.

Make-up: Sofia Alvarez Carreno
Modelling: Korlan Madi
Special credits: LEAM Luxury shop

EDUCATING THE CITIZEN

Elizabeth Laferrière

Laferrière is one of the seven designers commissioned by UQAM to each create a portrait for one of their faculties. Educating the Citizen introduces programmes of the Faculty of Education that cater for different age groups. Paint strokes on portraits tell stories of how education enhance the individual as well as society.

Client: Université du Québec à Montréal (UQAM)

MIXED MEDIA ILLUSTRATIONS

Prince Láuder

Finding new ways to interpret beauty and paying tribute to music and fashion icons such as David Bowie, Karl Lagerfeld, Daphne Groeneveld, Valeria Uscanga, Issa Lish and Andrea Carrazco, Láuder created this collection mixing photos, sketches, watercolour and typography.

DAVID BOWIE

i heart.

eal.

war isn't **CHIC.**

YOU ARE NOT WHAT YOU EAT

Jason Kerley

A mixed media project for KALTBLUT magazine's editorial about a girl and her grotesque and slimy feast of strange plants. Illustration style was a tribute to comic artist Tom Paterson's iconic delightfully disgusting approach on drawing.

Styling: Ellis Wood
Make-up & hair: Carmen Procopiuc
Modelling: Tatiana (D1)
Photo: Aleksandra Kingo

SCENT STORIES

Spiros Halaris Studio

An illustrated series for Citizen K magazine depicting perfume bottles and their botanic ingredients. Pale tones brushing onto sketches add an elegant note to the portrayal of fragrances.

Client: Citizen K magazine

AESOP

Spiros Halaris Studio

A photorealistic illustration series highlighting skincare brand Aesop's signature typographic packaging. Edgy watercolours add spice to the seemingly graphite sketches.

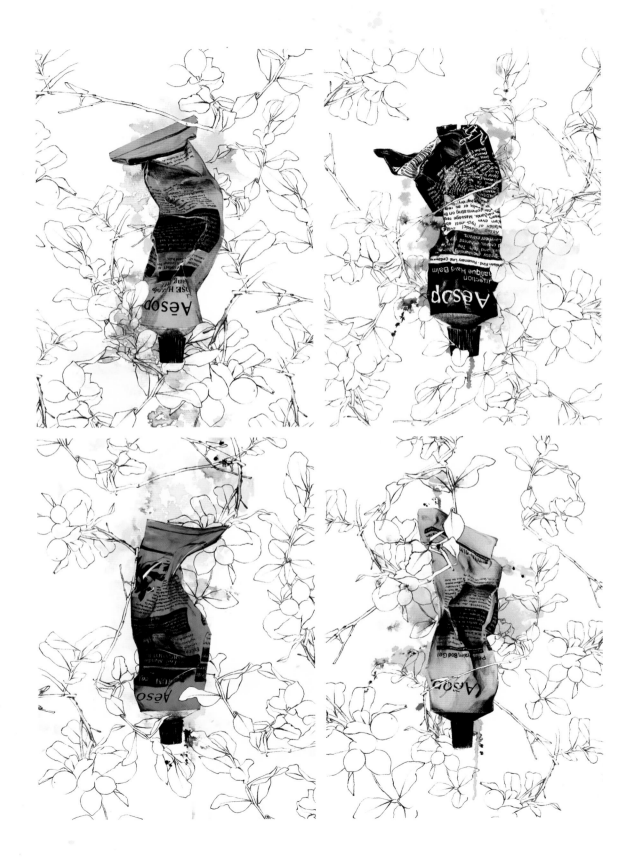

HKTDC DESIGN GALLERY

Sixstation Workshop

HKTDC Design Gallery is
a platform dedicated to
promoting local product
design. Promotional posters
commissioned by the gallery
are designed to celebrate "The
Grace of Creation."

Client: HKTDC Design Gallery

Designed by Benny Luk

Designed by Benny Luk

100%
HKDESIGNS

HKTDC
Design**gallery**
香港·設計廊

100%
HKDESIGNS

HKTDC
Design**gallery**
香港·設計廊

Designed by Benny Luk

100%
HKDESIGNS

HKTDC
Design**gallery**
香港·設計廊

Designed by Benny Luk

SILENT SHAPES
Oh Yeah Studio

A poster project that explores fluid shapes and graphic texture. The result is a metaphysical combination of enigmatic objects in an empty space.

BRANDS IN FULL BLOOM: SERIES I & II

Daryl Feril Studio

Not just another advertisment for luxury brands, the experimental poster series feature intricate foliage and blossoms closing in on big-name logotypes. Fine sketches filled the posters in the most resplendent fashion, while splashes of watercolour enhance depth and mood.

PAINT BALL

Marcel Christ Photography

Paint balls hit and burst on bottles
of male fragrances, a personal
project that uses beaming colours
to touch up packaging design.

BLURRED FACE

Yujiro Tada

The idea to create masks with watercolour came to artist Yujiro Tada's mind in a flash. Black and white portrait photos in low contrast wear masks of symmetric inkblot or random splatter in enhanced satuation, giving the subjects a carnivalesque look.

MANCHAS DE AGUA

Lucía Ares

Meaning "water spots," a series of abstract creatures are illustrated for WWF's advertising campaign "No Water No Life." The play of diluting watercolour with water enhances light and shade that contour the animals and remind the important role that water plays in human life.

Art direction: Raúl López, Aurora Hidalgo (Contrapunto BBDO)
Agency: Contrapunto BBDO
Client: WWF

SIN AGUA
NO HAY VIDA

SIN AGUA
NO HAY VIDA

TYPE
REVOLUTION

Calligraphy is the sum of strength and rhythm, while digital illustrations give words volume and forms. When new mediums and images replace ink, words acquire extra meanings that can be poetic and unpredictable.

DEPTHS

Eric Gorvin

Naming and poster design
for a group show featuring
experimental 3D work created
by students of Minneapolis
College of Art & Design. Layers
of white acrylic paint were
repeatedly applied to render
volume in letters emerging
from a white void.

*Client: Minneapolis College
of Art & Design
Special credits: STEAKMOB**

MCAD AT BI WORLDWIDE®

PRESENTS

DYLAN ADAMS
LUKE AXELSON
GRETCHEN BOOTH
DEREK ERNSTER
BRENNAN GASSER
CHRISTOPHER GASSER
NICHOLAS KOVATCH

FEBRUARY
TO
MARCH

CHELSEA LAPORTA
STEVEN LISTWON
IAN NYSTROM
PETER RA
JOSH RITENOUR
SEAN ROTH
ANDY SANDBERG

...Minneapolis College of Art and Design

4:30, 5:30, AND 6:30 SHUTTLE LEAVES MCAD
6:30 AND 7:30 VAN SHUTTLE RETURNS TO MCAD

7425 BUSH LAKE ROAD
EDINA, MN 55439

COMPLIMENTARY
FOOD & DRINK

DOOR PRIZES
IPAD 2, IPOD
& ITUNES $

GAUTE M. SORTLAND

Anti

Each painted using a different household object, from toothbrush to a cat's tail, the letters on the cover allude to the short stories inside, many derived from the comforts (and discomforts) at home. Subjects include parish priests and hedonists dealing with changes in life.

Client: Gaute M. Sortland, Det Norske Samlaget

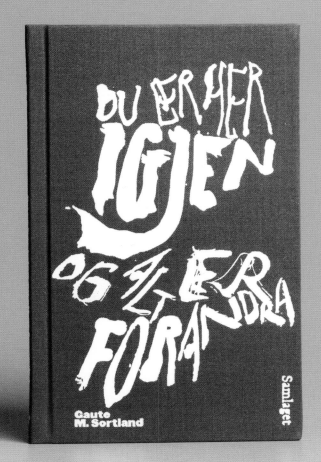

THE SUPERMARKET SERIES

Triboro

Hand-painted posters for the Great Poster Project hosted by New York-based bimonthly, Art on Paper. Typically loaded with colourful images and dramatic slogans, supermarket advertisements were re-imagined with witty, stylised text. The collection interpreted products like milk and cat wipes.

Client: Art on Paper Magazine

ILLUSTRATING "HONG KONG"

Don Mak

Special edition sleeve cover artwork for Creative City, a map-guide introducing Hong Kong from the local creatives' perspective. The result is a mix of the city's iconic cultural features such as vintage window grilles, antique gas lamps and fisheries, practised by Hong Kong's earliest residents.

Client: Creative City Hong Kong, Whitespace Hong Kong Limited

FLOW
Sawdust

Typographic exploration using acetate and acrylic paint. By dashing paint on transparent plastic stripes, Sawdust creates an illusion of movements and depth in the word as they raise and bend the strokes. Now the word literally "flows" in wavy lines.

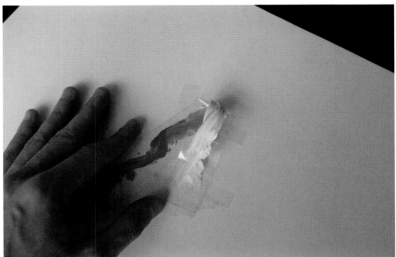

NIZAAM
AL
LAHOOT

VIA
NEGATIVA

XU XRI
GONG SHENG

CREATIO
EX
NIHILO

VIA
NEGATIVA

WU ZHONG
SHENG YOU

INK AND DESIGN
Sixstation Workshop

"Ink" is one of China's most important inventions and has profound influence on modern day design. "Nihility" depicted in the posters was a response to "Something out of Nothing," the exhibition theme of Ink and Design, organised by Dr. Kan Tai-keung and designers and curators from Japan, Taiwan and China.

Client: Ink and Design Exhibition

PLEASE! #08

Charlotte Delarue

Paintings for PLEASE! Magazine
with art directions from
Leslie David. To celebrate the
magazine's 5th birthday, 12
artists and designers were
invited and given a carte
blanche to reinterpret the
publication's archive images.
This piece reworked image from
issue 08 with textured paint.

FUSION OF MIRAGE

ALL WILL COME INTO ON
2013 / 03 / 08

意
境
·
融
徹

Fusion Of Mirage

意

Calligraphy By:
Lok Ng

Design By:
Lok Ng

Creative By:
Sek Team & awt inc.

Photography By:
Yuu Auyeung

©awt design inc.
www.awtdi.com

ONE DRE
AND
ONE LIGH

ALL WILL COME INTO ONE
2013 / 03 / 08

一
念
·
生
花

One Dream One Light

念

Calligraphy By:
Lok Ng

Design By:
Lok Ng

Creative By:
Sek Team & awt inc.

Photography By:
Yuu Auyeung

©awt design inc.
www.awtdi.com

COME INTO ONE

awt design inc.

Come into one presents philosophical concepts that sum up the meanings of design in a new era. As "Fusion Of Mirage," "One Dream and One Light" and "Shape Of A Shadow," the idea of "Balance" and "Integration" is visualised as Eastern and Western aesthetics (in ink calligraphy and illustrations) "come into one."

Photo: Yuu Auyeung
Client: Seek Strategy Co., Ltd

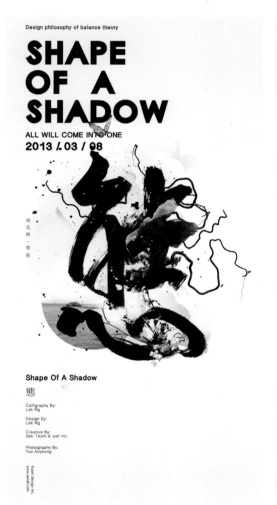

Design philosophy of balance theory

SHAPE OF A SHADOW

ALL WILL COME INTO ONE
2013 / 03 / 08

Shape Of A Shadow

態

Calligraphy By:
Lok Ng

Design By:
Lok Ng

Creative By:
Sek Team & awt inc.

Photography By:
Yuu Auyeung

@awt design inc.
www.awt8.com

Design philosophy of balance theory

ALL WILL COME INTO ONE

{ Fusion Of Mirage
One Dream One Light
Shape Of A Shadow }

2013 / 03 / 08

ALL WILL COME INTO ONE

和合

Calligraphy By:
Lok Ng

Design By:
Lok Ng

Creative By:
Sek Team & awt inc.

Photography By:
Yuu Auyeung

@awt design inc.
www.awt8.com

1

2

CAN HUA/FLOATING

awt design inc.

Marrying illustration, calligraphy
and photography by Yasumasa
Yonehara, Can Hua (1 & 2) suggests
an alternative angle to contemplate
and appreciate the beauty of women.
Floating (3) seeks to portray what life
is in this fleeting world.

Photo & client: Yasumasa Yonehara
Modelling: Yuki Sanada, Aoi Tsukasa

Photography : Yasumasa Yonehara
Creative Design : Lok Ng
Model : Aoitsukasa

LOVELINESS

awt design inc.

The charm of woman is compared
to the grace of flowering. Calligraphy,
typeface and illustrations were
juxtaposed with Yasumasa Yonehara's
photography to demonstrate an
alternative angle to contemplate the
beauty of women.

Photo & client: Yasumasa Yonehara
Modelling: Aoi Tsukasa

Photography : Yasumasa Yonehara
Creative Design : Lok Ng
Model : Aoitsukasa

IMMIT LOVE

awt design inc.

Studio work probing into truths in real life. By framing drifting ink with a heart symbolic of love, Immit Love expresses that "love" can at once give people strength and pain. Black and white, definite and formless — there are always two sides to the equation.

Client: LK Coffee Shop

UNKNOWN

awt design inc.

Studio work that takes on abstraction to invite spectators to understand things thoroughly by observing the surface and feel it by instinct at the same time.

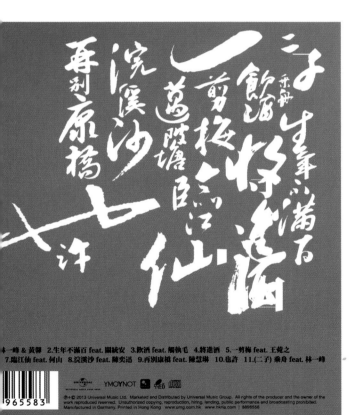

CHAPTERS – ALEX FUNG

COMMONROOOM

A figurative expression of affection referencing Chinese literary classics within western music framework, Chapters is a contemporary fusion of tradition and modernity. The concept is suggested in the mix of powerful movements restrained by a grey tone.

Photo: Wing Shya
Client: Universal Music Ltd.

RURUBU

Nobuhiro Sato, Haley Friesen

The strength and movements of ballet dancers photographed by Haley Friesen was thoroughly interpreted in Japanese character's slashes and twists. The characters "Ru-ru-bu" inscribed by artist Nobuhiro Sato with heavy brush strokes and sporadic ink splatters essentially means "to dance and flow slowly."

Modelling: Kathleen Legassick, Meaghan Silva

PIANO SERIES 2014

Sara Westermann

Characteristic of piano's keys, a reduced colour scheme was paired with thick-stroke letters hand-written with large-tip markers. The huge letter "Y" in reversed colour introduced Yundi Li, the pianist to perform at the annual Piano Cycle presented by Casa da Música.

Client: Casa da Música

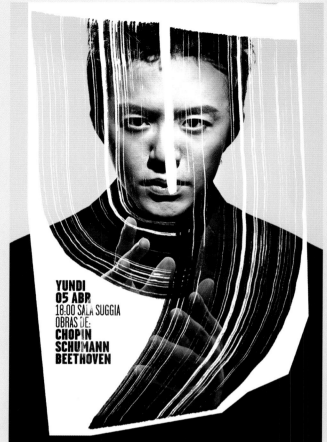

YUNDI
05 ABR
18:00 SALA SUGGIA
OBRAS DE:
CHOPIN
SCHUMANN
BEETHOVEN

YUNDI
05 ABR
18:00 SALA SUGGIA
OBRAS DE:
CHOPIN
SCHUMANN
BEETHOVEN

ILLEST

Hello Tello

Experimental type treatment
imagining splashed ink spelling
"Illest" for a split second,
captured in a spray booth
environment. Illest is an urban
fashion brand owned by
designer's friend, Mark Arcenal.

*Special credits: Mark Arcenal
(Fatlace)*

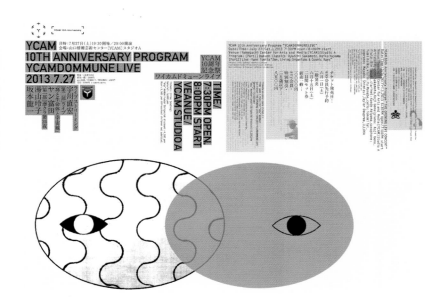

YCAM 10TH ANNIVERSARY

Rikako Nagashima

Programme flyers and posters for Yamaguchi Center for Arts and Media's (YCAM) tenth birthday. Multi-directional text arrangement visualises the interconnection between "art," "environment" and "life," in response to the theme "Yamaguchi Art and Environment for Tomorrow."

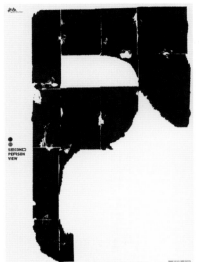

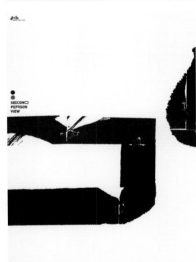
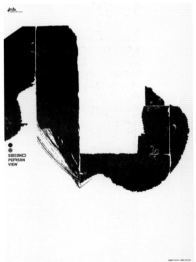

INGENUITY FOLLOWS NATURE

Wang Zhi-Hong Studio

Posters collection for Interdisciplinary
Creative Works on Asia's Cultural
Creativity Exhibition, held as part of
Taipei World Design Expo 2011. Visual
elements present how a message can
be interpreted by individuals by shuffling
the components of an original work.

Calligraphy: Tong Yang-Tze
Client: Interdisciplinary Creative Works

ORIGINAL MUSIC WORKSHOP

SKYFUL

EDITED BY
WQXR Q2 MUSIC
CLAIRE CHASE
ERIC LAMB
TALEA ENSEMBLE
TONY ARNOLD
KINAN AZMEH
CORNELIUS DUFALLO
MAGOS HERRERA
ERIKA HARRSCH
JAVIER LIMÓN

JULIAN WACHNER
MARIO DIAZ DE LEON
BERNHARD LANG

SEPTEMBER 13TH, 2012
7:00PM

AT THE GREENE SPACE

ORIGINAL MUSIC WORKSHOP

SONG PRESERVATIONISTS

IN COLLABORATION WITH
CARNEGIE HALL'S MUSICAL
EXCHANGE PROGRAM
CELSO DUARTE
MAGOS HERRERA

NOVEMBER 20TH, 2012
7:00PM

AT THE GREENE SPACE

ORIGINAL MUSIC WORKSHOP

VOCAL ELECTROFOLK

IN COLLABORATION WITH
HARARE INTERNATIONAL
FESTIVAL OF THE ARTS
DAVID KRAKAUER
JEFFREY ZEIGLER
HELGA DAVIS
NETSAYI

MARCH 16TH, 2013
7:00PM

AT THE GREENE SPACE

ORIGINAL MUSIC WORKSHOP

VARIATIONS IN FOUR HANDS

IN COLLABORATION WITH
SOUND RES INTERNATIONAL
RESIDENCY PROGRAM
ALESSIO BAX
LUCILLE CHUNG
LUCA TARANTINO

JANUARY 21TH, 2013
7:00PM

AT THE GREENE SPACE

OMW POSTERS

Mogollon

Gig posters for Original Music Workshop (OMW), a non-profit that champions musicians and composers at the heart of Brooklyn. On top of a bouncy logotype, also devised by Mogollon, free-form ornaments and a duo-tone scheme cohere with OMW's focus on experimentation and artistic progress.

Client: Original Music Workshop (OMW), BUREAU V

POETS' POZNAŃ FESTIVAL NEWSPAPER

Marcin Markowski

Poets' Poznań is a biennial
international poetry festival
in Poznań, Poland. Visual
identification of its 2013 edition
danced around a letter to bridge
poetry, literature and the event.

Client: Zamek Cultural Center

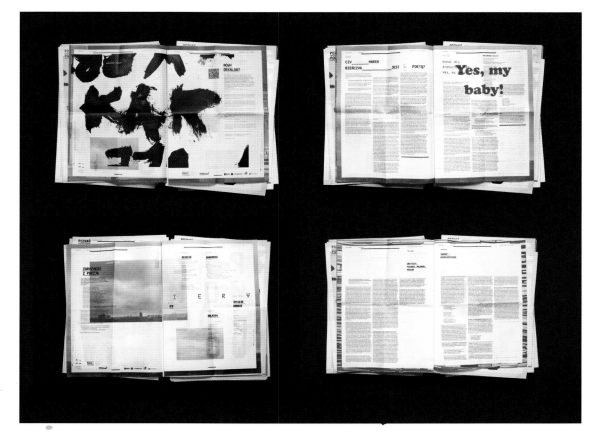

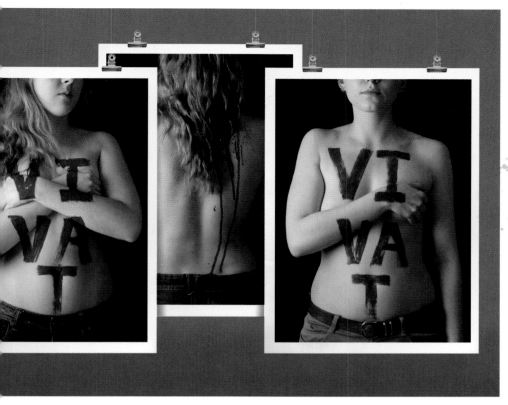

VIVAT LA DANSE! 2013

Les produits de l'épicerie

Communications for a dance festival presented by Le Vivat in France. Individuals of different sexes and ages were photographed to express "diversity" and highlight "body" as the focal point. The blue paint is metaphor for the art of body movements, just as colour invades the bodies.

Photo: Charly Desoubry

1

V!TOR
Pyramid Studio

Invitation for V!tor, a Porto-based street wear brand. Brimming with colours and paint, the design beautifully transfers the brand's Spring/Summer 2013 collection's intense palette into the cards. The colour theme expands to business card and lookbook. (1)

ADANA TWINS & KOLLEKTIV TURMSTRASSE
Pyramid Studio

Gig Posters for the Australian record label and artist management agency Lucid Dreaming Productions. Marbled patterns, colours and distortions visually described the live music of electronic music bands Adana Twins and Kollectiv Turmstrasse. (2 & 3)

Client: Lucid Dreaming Productions

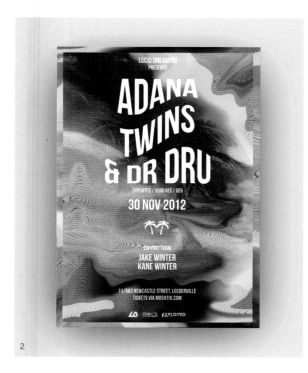

2

3

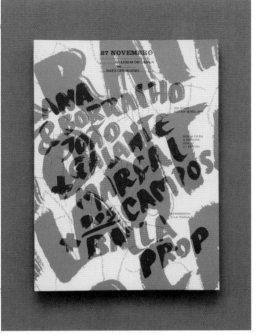

DAYS OFF SOUND

Sara Westermann

Held under Blue Summer Festival in Lagos, south Portugal, Days Off Sound is a unique meeting point for sound artists. Westermann translates the improvised nature of speech and sound onto fold-out posters, on which hand-writing serves as both graphical and informative element.

Insert: Joana Macedo
Client: NEC (Núcleo de Experimentação Coreográfica)

TANGIBLE
DROPS

Touch a paint drop without getting stained. Whether it's a rug or hardened polyurethane foam chair, these lighthearted artefacts create tangible illusion and bring impossibilities to real life. Realising naturalistic details challenge makers to think outside the box.

SYMMETRICA

Richard Blake

A personal project of Blake to capture symmetrical patterns of Rorschach inkblot test by laser cut headpieces. Infusing strong graphic element in fashion design, these wearable sculptures are helpful to examine and highlight human facial features.

Photo: Kamie Lynn Robinson

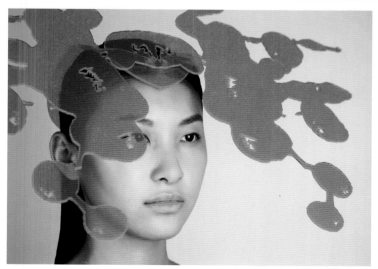

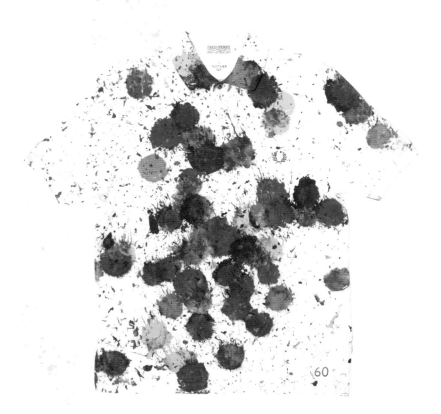

60 SWINGS FOR FRED PERRY
Mother Design

Sixty contributors were tapped to revive Fred Perry's original 1952 polo shirt for its 60th birthday. Mother Design's token of respect was expressed in 60 swings, hitting paint-soaked tennis balls against the shirt 60 times to give it a final touch. The process was documented and is available on the agency's Vimeo page.

Client: Fred Perry

HÀBITATS I CONTRA-HÀBITATS

Mucho

"Environments and Counter-environments" is an attempt to reassess the visionary possibilities suggested by the exhibition "Italy: The New Domestic Landscape" held at MoMA in 1972. The play between plastic's liquid and solid state as signage is a means to highlight its role in innovation of architecture and design in 1970's.

Materials: GRUPO IRPEN
Client: Disseny Hub Barcelona
Special credits: emiliana design studio

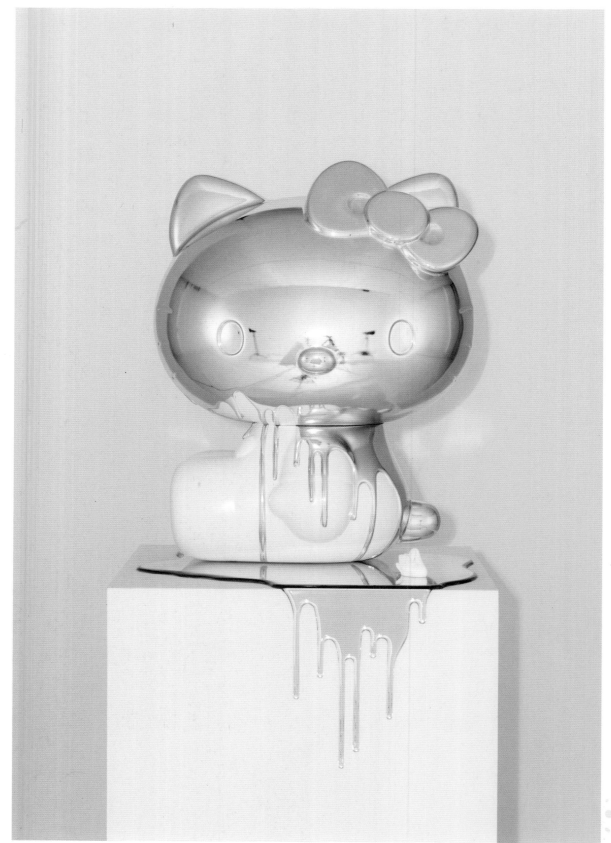

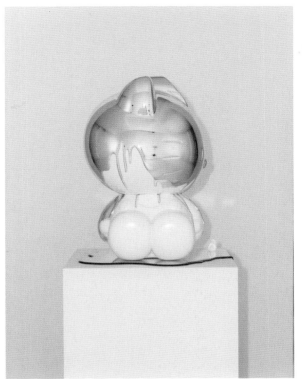

HOUSE OF HELLO KITTY
Rikako Nagashima

Japanese artist and art director Rikako Nagashima "pours" her fond Mizukagami (water mirror) element down the celebrated cartoon character for this charitable exhibition. Her sculpture piece is among nine created by local artists to benefit the Tohoku earthquake relief.

1

2

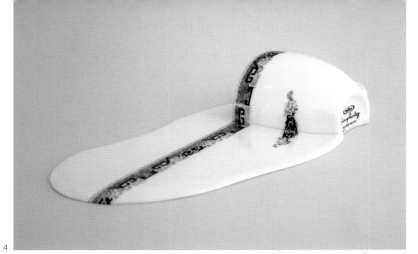

4

5

NOMAD PATTERNS AND BROKEN THINGS

Livia Marin

A sculpture series by London-based Chilean artist Livia Marin in which exquisite-looking ceramics experience a visual melt down, with meticulous embellishments still paradoxically intact. Liquidity has allowed Marin to explore between form and formlessness.

1 © Livia Marin, Nomad Patterns, 2012 / Collection of Canterbury Museum, Christchurch, New Zealand
2 & 3 © Livia Marin, Nomad Patterns, 2012
4 & 5 © Livia Marin, Broken Things, 2009

3

FORM FOLLOWS FOAM

Therese Granlund

A collection of furniture overpowered by polyurethane, in which this plain Jane of all materials become the star with its organic form and fancy colours. Through this material-oriented project, Granlund confronts the obsession with perfection in design and control in industrial manufacturing.

Special credits: BASF

NEVER TOO MUCH
Kueng Caputo

Represented by Salon94
in partnership with Rudy
Weissenberg, Never Too Much
is an array of benches, stools
and bowls that celebrates the
experimentation of material
and colour. Under the guise of
buoyant hand-painted fleck and
speck are soft Italian leather seats,
strong enamel base and bowls in
eccentric shapes.

Photo: Suter Caputo

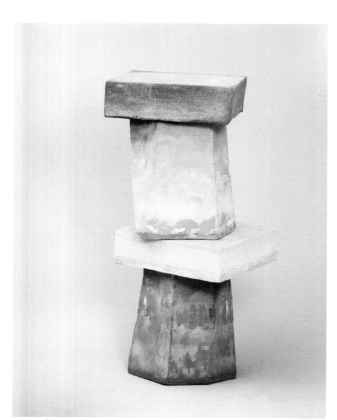

SAND CHAIR
Kueng Caputo

Represented by Salon94, these chalky-textured stools are created as a project to experiment pigments. These curious-looking seating objects are made out of sand and mortar, then fine-tuned by hammer and chisel out of casting moulds, sturdy enough to add colours to both in-and outdoor environments.

Photo: Suter Caputo

ÉCUME

Ferréol Babin

Literally translated "foam," Écume is overlaid with distinctive rings. In addition to pine or beech wood grain, an undirected colouring process has given these stools and tables their unique marbled patterns, and different colour combinations yield distinctive characters. The entire collection is handmade by Babin.

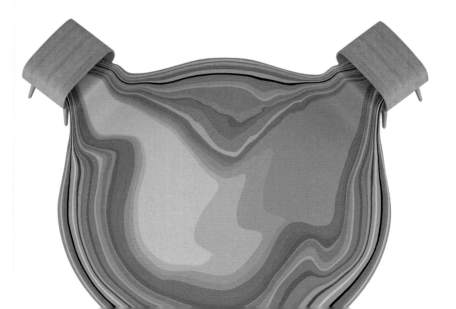

CONFLUENTIA

Bina Baitel

An award-wining piece at an international contest of contemporary tapestry in 2012, Confluentia is where furniture and the textile art join as one. Stretching 3.4 metres far and wide between two wooden reliefs is a contour map interlaced by threads and colours — a micro-landscape in the living room.

Client: Aubusson International City of Tapestry

TARAH

Bina Baitel

Meaning "to throw down" in Arabic, Tarah is a self-contained living space consisting a padded surface that can be rolled up and buckled itself around the attaching wrought iron side table embellished with gold leaf.

Client: NextLevel Gallery

SHAGREEN
Bina Baitel

A seamless combination of
shagreen lampshade and
leather desk pad by quality
French handcraft, this side
lamp re-interprets interaction
between light and material,
with the latter component
playing on materialisation of
light's trajectory.

Client: NextLevel Gallery
Photo: Florian Kleinefenn

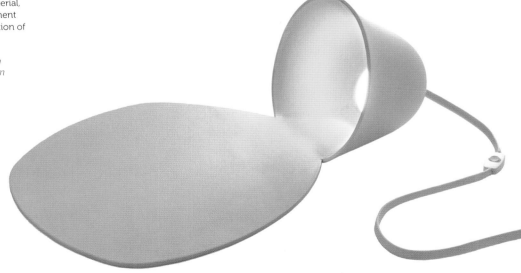

GRIMM

Bina Baitel

Named after the Grimm brothers, creators of Snow White and the Magic Mirror, Baitel wishes to conjure uncanny images with this mirror-lamp. Lampshade in blown glass, reflecting bulb and the flat surface of mirror are instruments essential to conduct this game of light and image.

Client: NextLevel Gallery

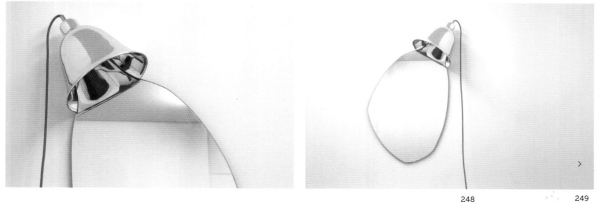

WHO'S WHO

ACRE
P. 034-035

Operating from the industrial heartlands of Singapore, ACRE is idea crafters, T Y Zheng and Jason Song. Likening themselves to "a plot of arable land", ACRE promises to offer a good ground where untapped potential and possibilities within the seed of every good idea flourish at its best. Specialising in art direction, branding and advertising, the creative agency is committed to offering innovative solutions for businesses.

AL HAZWANI, AMIN & SANTA, PHILIP
P. 048-049

Two young designers from Italy, Hazwani and Santa are trying to specialise in their respective interests through a wide range of projects.

AMORE
P. 096

Amore is an agency with leading-edge tools for brand innovation, design creation and creative culture.

ANAGRAMA
P. 022-023

Anagrama's services reach the entire branding spectrum from strategic consulting to fine tuning brand objectives for clients, logotype, peripherals and illustration. Besides the history and experience with brand development, the agency is also experts in the design and development of objects, spaces and multimedia projects.

ANTI
P. 116-119, 193

A Norwegian multidisciplinary design studio believes in the power of interference. The team works to find new ways interacting with audience. Due to the bombardment of communication for consumers at all angles, Anti always creates something novel and unexpected in order to grab viewers' attention.

APEX STUDIO
P. 128

Founder and art director Tiago Machado believes that process is as important as the final form where intensity of expression, value of work and professional standard combined. From aspired illustrator to visual graphic communicator, Machado is influenced by American comic art and the obsession of having the final product as an collectible object.

ARES, LUCÍA
P. 188-189

Born in Asturias, 1987, Ares moved to Madrid and graduated in Fine Arts at the Complutense University. Since then, she began to exhibit individually and collectively. Ares is also active in advertising and has won numerous awards in the field including two Silvers in the Art Director Club of Europe Awards. In 2013, Ares was a finalist in the BMW National Prize for Painting.

ARTILLO, ERNESTO
P. 158-161

Born in Málaga, Spain in 1987, Artillo's interest is to work on images as a form, using trends as a pathway for creating new concepts. Having fashion as one of the main creative platform, where Artillo collaborates with international designers, brands and magazines, he has also exhibited his personal artwork in several cities like Saint Patersburg, Mumbai and Madrid.

ARTLESS INC.
P. 091-095

Established in 2000 by Shun Kawakami, the interdisciplinary design and consulting firm works across all media including brand design, visual and corporate identity, advertising, packaging, product, video and motion graphics etc. The studio has won several prestigious international awards including CANNES Gold Lions, NY ADC, D&AD and The London International Award.

AWT DESIGN INC.
P. 200-205

arts worth thing design inc. is an independent and creative company focuses on planning, market strategy and concept design. The team believes brand image is very important as the traditional communication channels to disperse and increase new media for their clients. awt's services include strategy and media planning, graphic design, illustration, and website construction.

BABIN, FERRÉOL
P. 242-243

Born in Dijon, France in 1987, Babin studied design in France and Japan and is now working at Fabrica in Italy. His main focus is on lighting engineering design and he is extremely interested in interaction between users and objects. His projects are always based on an awareness of function and rationale, teamed with a poetic, emotional aspect.

BAITEL, BINA
P. 244-248

Born in Paris in 1977 and graduated from the National School of Architecture La Villette in 2002, Baitel works across a broad range of sectors including furniture, lighting, architecture, consumer goods, art direction, and space installations. The winner of the VIA Creation Award in 2008, Baitel inaugurates her first solo show at the NextLevel Galerie in 2010 and recieved

The City of Paris Grand Prize for Creation and the First Prize of the International City of Aubusson tapestry in 2012. Currently based in Paris, Baitel cultivates experimentation and simplicity to transform concepts into objects and spaces.

BLAKE, RICHARD
P. 226-227

A visual designer and creative consultant working in art direction, branding, editorial, and product design.

BÜRO UEBELE VISUELLE KOMMUNIKATION
P. 081

Founded in 1996 by Andreas Uebele, the agency is active in all areas of visual communications, with the focus on visual identity, signage and wayfinding systems, corporate communications and exhibitions. In recent years the agency's work has been honoured with more than 300 national and international awards.

CHOCOLATE EDITIONS BY MARY & MATT
P. 012-013

Chocolate Editions by Mary & Matt is a celebration of candy bars as a perfect pop object. Launched in their home kitchen as gifts for friends and family, it quickly grew into a full line of deliciously artful candies. Mary & Matt use the highest quality ingredients and craft their chocolate bars in small, handmade batches. They always have their eyes and taste buds open for surprising inspirations.

COAST
P. 082-083

A multidisciplinary creative agency with more than 15 years of experience in brand creation and communication design for all sectors and disciplines - offline and online. Opened in 1999 as a design practice focused on graphic design and visual creativity, Coast is now a global agency with an international network of creatives working on different levels of brand consultancy - from working hand in hand with clients on strategy to the development of custom-made creative ideas.

COCOLIA
P. 010-011, 077, 105

A graphic design studio focuses on corporate identity, graphic communication, art direction, editorial, web, illustration, and art projects. They believe having a close relationship with clients is the way to get best possible results. Cocolia also elaborates personal projects where they have absolute freedom on implementing new techniques and visual impact.

COMMONROOOM
P. 206-207

The Hong Kong-based design studio is expertised in producing bold and memorable graphic design and art direction with a bespoke approach. The studio works on a diverse range of projects for clients big and small including Universal Music, Lane Crawford, Wing Shya and a host of smaller independents.

CORRADO, KEVIN
P. 144-145

A fine art photographer producing art from all around Connecticut, Corrado is currently finishing his senior year at SASD obtaining a BFA in graphic design.

DAILY . J
P. 026-027

A design group consists of Jaehee Park, Jieun Lee, and Jooyeon Ha pursuing beauty in daily life through a variety of research, enjoyment of everyday life and experimentation.

DARYL FERIL STUDIO
P. 180-183

The Philippine-based freelance illustrator, artist and graphic designer works on projects ranging from fashion and advertising campaigns to illustrations and textile patterns, packaging and visual merchandising graphics both digital and in print. Shortly after gratuated in 2012, Feril has worked with big names like DFS Group and Tiger Beer Singapore. His work is featured in international art magazines such as Computer Arts and Digital Arts.

DAVID, LESLIE
P. 154-157

Born to creative parents who run a poster business, David saw herself as a freelancer quite early on, during her studies at Ecole des Arts Decoratifs in Strasbourg, where she started taking illustration jobs for magazines and later joined petronio associates as a junior art director in 2006. Currently an independent art director, graphic designer and illustrator, David's goal is to broaden her creative experience clients from diverse fields.

DELARUE, CHARLOTTE
P. 199

Living and working in Paris, the illustrator works mainly on the music field and has worked with Surface To Air and Justice.

DEMIAN CONRAD DESIGN
P. 040-041

Founded in 2007, the multidisciplinary studio works mainly in the cultural field and the leisure industry focusing on events communication and visual identity. Based in Lausanne and Bellinzona, the team is always keen to work with clients who would like to play a full role in the creative process.

DESIGNERS UNITED
P. 130-131

An award winning, multidisciplinary design firm based in Thessaloniki, Greece. The company works for a diverse range of international clients across various industries, scales and budgets such as Volvo, Euroleague and Adidas. Their work encompasses creative direction, branding and identity systems, book and magazine design, web design and development, illustration, print collateral and social-media/public-relations needs.

DHARANI BASSOLS & MONTSE GALBANY
P. 120

Born in 1989 in Barcelona, Bassols is a graphic designer, and photographer grew up in a multicultural atmosphere of Spanish and German traditions. Galbany is a graphic designer and illustrator from Barcelona.

DOERIG, ASTRID
P. 088-089

A Swiss graphic designer based at Zurich. Doerig's passion is to experiment and work with different materials to develop art and designs including websites, flyers, corporate designs.

EHRENSTRÅHLE & WÅGNERT
P. 014

A young design agency in Stockholm focuses on brand identity, packaging design and concepts for films. The team strives to create an all-embracing visual impact for clients, while at the same time ensuring that each element feels unique with meaning and depth.

EL SEÑOR GÓMEZ & SRTA. SWALLOW
P. 097

Working under the moniker of El Señor Gómez & Srta. Swallow, Iván Gómez and Laia Delgado have been working together for two years. From Barcelona, although mainly working overseas, the graphic duo is specialised in music industry but also enjoy working for other fields.

FREGON, ALEX
P. 076

A designer and illustrator based in Melbourne, Australia. Fregon's work covers corporate identity and branding, editorial design, web design, illustration and finished art, both digital and traditional. Passionate to draw, Fregon also designs for music including the development of album and poster art.

GAWIN, MARTA
P. 070-073

A multidisciplinary graphic designer specialises in visual identity, sign system, poster, information, exhibition and editorial design. Since her MA in Graphic Design at the Academy of Fine Arts, Katowice in 2011, Gawin has been working as a freelancer for cultural institutions and commercial organisations. Her design approach is conceptual, logical and content-driven. What's more, she treats graphic design as a field of visual research and formal experiments.

GHOST DESIGN
P. 126-127

A multidisciplinary design agency located in Stavanger, Norway. Specialised in graphic design, industrial design and digital media along with other associated areas, Ghost's approach is user-friendly and functional. Work closely with clients and their expanded network, the team believes design is a strategic and important factor in creating strong brands and good user experiences.

GORVIN, ERIC
P. 192

Designer, art director, and lettersmith based in Minneapolis and Los Angeles. With a broad range of aptitude art and music, Gorvin works on a wide diversity of projects ranging from custom typography, to video shooting and editing, screen printing posters and apparels, as well as to running a brand.

GRANLUND, THERESE
P. 236-237

A freelance designer based in Stockholm, Sweden, Granlund mastered at the Design Academy in Eindhoven in 2012. The interest for functionality and the interface between industry and the human perception is central for her design. She creates objects with expressive value raising questions about its being and making.

GRONGAARD ART & DESIGN STUDIO
P. 038-039

Founded by Mette Grøngaard, the studio is driven by the idea of using techniques from art to create unique and vibrant graphic design solutions for brands, events and campaigns. Traditional techniques like splashes and drips of ink, thin accurate lines of pencils are also involved to express mood and give presence to design solution.

HELLO TELLO
P. 212-213

An American designer originally from The Bay Area but now resides in Los Angeles, Hello Tello specialises in storyboards and style frames for commercials, films, and games. His clients include NFL, Nike, Discovery, Imaginary Forces, Brand New School, Psyop, and The Mill to name a few.

HERR, AGNES & ELEK, GITA
P. 062-065

Two designers from Hungary. Now based in Budapest, graphic designer Herr graduated at Eszterházy Károly College in Eger with special interests in graphic design, identity, typography, branding and web design.

KARHUNEN, LEO
P. 079

An independent art director, Karhunen creates identities, concepts and campaigns across multiple media.

KERLEY, JASON
P.170-171

Based in London, Kerley is a freelance visual designer and musician with a background in illustration. Also a curator and visual and conceptual artist, Kerley's work tends to be collaborative in nature and comprises of spatial, screen and print based projects.

KIM, DEREK
P. 114-115

A artist and graphic designer based in San Francisco, USA who specialises in art direction, illustration and typography, Kim's main approach to design is to fuse the disciplines of art and design together, creating visual conversations with his audience.

KING, OLIVIA & ANDREASSEN, SEBASTIAN
P. 052-053

Designer and illustrator King is passionate about typography, branding, illustration and language while Andreassen is a designer, co-founder and creative director of Dandy Magazine who constantly seek a diversity and variety through the people and ideas that influence what he creates. His work is strongly typographic and fiercely conceptual. Both based in Sydney, Australia, the two were an Emerging Talent finalist for the Desktop Create Awards in 2012 and 2013 respectively. King also received an AGDA award that year and was shortlisted for the AgIdeas NewStar award in 2013.

KRUSE JØRGENSEN, HENRIETTE
P. 015

Specialised in visual communication within the cultural field, Kruse is expanding her skills to interaction and social design through a variety of projects. The freelance designer is now based in Copenhagen, Denmark.

KUENG CAPUTO
P. 238-241

Both studied industrail design at ZHDK, Zurich, Sarah Kueng and Lovis Caputo collaborate since 2006 on innovative projects exploring mundane materials and environments to exercise and reflect high design and architectural concepts. Their work evokes the uncertain boundaries between the visual arts, design, architecture, and popular culture. The duo has been invited to museums, galleries, and design and art fairs worldwide including venues in Zurich, Basel, Milan, Cape Town, Seoul, Tokyo, and New York.

LAFERRIÈRE, ELIZABETH
P. 166-167

Laferrière is a graphic designer and art director based in Canada.

LARSSON, VERONIKA
P. 030-031

Born in 1991, Larsson is currently studing visual communication at Beckmans College of Design in Stockholm, Sweden.

LÁUDER, PRINCE
P. 168-169

With a background in philosophy and visual arts, Láuder's work is defined by a game between fashion and art that constructs with different techniques and elements. Through experimentation results in a series of illustrations where female beauty is the main protagonist, his work has positioned itself as one of the youngest artists with high impact on fashion internationally, winning several awards and accolading around the world. Láuder's clients includes major brands and publishers such as Givenchy, Kipling, Elle, Vogue and many more.

LES PRODUITS DE L'ÉPICERIE
P. 220-221

A french graphic design studio based in Lille, France. Specialised in graphic and visual design mainly for the cultural field, the studio creates to stimulate imagination and interpretation with new reflexion through original photographic, illustrative or graphic images.

LEYVA CABALLERO, DIEGO
P. 060

Leyva is a designer of visual information creating concepts and design experiences to get exquisite results.

LOREM IPSUM STUDIO
P. 066-069

Lorem Ipsum is an independent design studio based in Belgrade, Serbia. They specialises in graphic design, typography and illustration. Lorem Ipsum emerged out of the need to rethink design out of the lifestyle context, as far removed from the logic of market as possible.

MAK, DON
P. 195

Born and bought up in Hong Kong, Mak's passion and artistry bloomed early and joined the local comic talents at 16. Graduated in Visual Communication from The Hong Kong Polytechnic University in 2009, Mak has since been illustrating freelance for magazines, publishers and advertising agencies. He's also a member of the Hong Kong Society of Illustrators since 2004.

MARCEL CHRIST PHOTOGRAPHY
P.184-185

After graduating with honors from the Academy of Photography in Amsterdam, the Netherlands, Christ shot for clients such as Sony, Samsung, Evian, L'Oreal, Nike, New Balance, Coca Cola and Stella Artois. The photographer is known for his mastery of still lifes which lend an unmistakable life-force to ordinary objects, transforming jewels, shoes and liquids into sleek art forms. Christ, who divides his time between New York and his native Amsterdam, also makes time to shoot for Details, ELLE, City Magazine, New York Times Magazine and Instyle.

MARICOR/MARICAR
P. 104

The studio of fraternal twins Maricor and Maricar Manalo based in Sydney. The duo is specialised in illustration, embroidery and papercut lettering working mostly with needle, thread, fabric and paper. Their work has exhibited in Australia and internationally.

MARIN, LIVIA
P. 234-235

The London-based Chilean artist has been knwon for her large-scale installations and the appropriation of mass-produced and consumer objects. Central to her work is a trope of estrangement that works to reverse an excess of familiarity engendered in the life of the everyday and by the dictates of the marketplace. Marin has exhibited widely both in her native Chile and internationally.

MARKEVIČIUS, TOMAS
P. 162-163

Graduated in BA Creative Industries at Vilnius Gediminas Technical University in 2012, Markevičius is a graphic and motion designer based in Vilnius, Lithuania working in various creative fields ranging from fashion to photography, illustration, graphic design, motion graphics and animation.

MARKOWSKI, MARCIN
P. 218-219

The founder of a sole proprietorship, Yo studio, the graphic designer focuses to work on visual identification, cultural frame of events, publication design, typography and poster design.

MCFARLINE, DAVID
P. 087

Now a freelance graphic designer based in London who spent five years working for the multi award-winning design studio Spin, McFarline runs the record label Noncollective which also hosts mixes for some of the world's most eclectic DJs and music lovers.

MILENKOVIC, BRATISLAV
P. 080

An illustrator and graphic designer currently living and working in Belgrade, Serbia, Milenkovic graduated in illustration in Belgrade. He works for various clients such as The New York Times, Financial Times, Wired, Computer Arts, Mikser Festival, Museum of Contemporary Art Belgrade, etc. His works have been successfully exhibited throughout Europe, as well as published in numerous publications.

MOGOLLON
P. 216-217

A design duo based in New York City by Mónica Brand and Francisco López. They teamed up in 2004 to start Mogollón and work on a range of projects, including art direction, graphic design, illustration, set design and multimedia design for the music, fashion, film, entertainment and art industries.

MOTHER DESIGN
P. 228-229

Creating fully integrated brand communications that are anchored in strategy, culture and design, Mother Design is a design and branding group within advertising agency Mother New York making identity systems, books, billboards, apps, films, websites, packages, whiskey, political t-shirts, environments and more.

MUCHO
P. 230-231

A visual communications and graphics studio expertised in art direction, strategic and corporate identity, editorial design, packaging, graphic communications, digital design and motion graphics.

MULLIGAN, CLARA
P. 050-051

Started out at the early age of six as the CEO of "Trends", a puffy paint t-shirt business, Mulligan received her MFA in graphic design from Rhode Island School of Design, USA. Besides running her own studio specialising in identity and interactive design. Mulligan also co-directs and manages the design department at Creature. Her clients inlcudes Zune, Nike, Microsoft Windows, K2, and Seattle Best Coffee. Her work has been featured in Communication Arts, Print Magazine, and Type Director's Club, etc.

MUSTONEN, SANTTU
P. 146-147

An artist interested in colorful mud, moving images, 3D design, art direction and contemporary illustration.

NAGASHIMA, RIKAKO
P. 108-113, 214, 232-233

Born in 1980, Nagashima graduated in Visual Communication Design at Musashino Art University in 2003. The art director and designer's work covers a wide range of areas including signage design, advertising, branding, spatial design, product design, film production, and music video. The award winner and youngest member of ADC has started her own brand "Human_Nature" in 2013.

NB
P. 106-107

An award-winning, multidisciplinary branding and communication studio established in 1997, NB works hard to find the 'great idea' that each project needs, and follows it up with clear thinking and crafted expression. Owned and creatively directed by Nick Finney and Alan Dye, NB works with the best people to suit their clients' needs, and provides solutions that are beautiful, effective and appropriate.

NEO NEO
P. 056-057

A Geneva based graphic design studio founded in 2010 by Thuy-An Hoang and Xavier Erni, Neo Neo is active in the cultural field working for museums, galleries, theaters, film festivals, etc. They create contemporary solutions with a focus on typography and direct messages.

NEWMAN, ADRIAN
P. 090

Newman's analytical approach to design is what pushes his solutions into a meaningful direction. He creates with a focus on the cyclical nature of business and strive for harmony between the client and the artifact.

NICHOLSON, TAYLOR
P. 029

A graphic designer working in Cleveland, Ohio, Nicholson graudated in Graphic Design at Antoinette Westphal College of Media Arts and Design at Drexel University in Philadelphia, USA. Her specialties lie in print design, which consist mainly of packaging, book design, branding and typography. But she is also interested in all mediums of design, and enjoys designing for interactive and web experiences as well.

NON-FORMAT
P. 086

Established in London in 2000 by Kjell Ekhorn and Jon Forss, the two-man team works on a diverse range of projects including art direction, design, illustration and custom typography for a list of international brands. Forss relocated to Minneapolis, USA and, in 2009, Ekhorn returned to his native Norway. Skype™ becomes the bridge for them to work together on every project.

OH YEAH STUDIO
P. 178-179

Set up by Hans Christian Øren and Christina Magnussen in 2008 who met each other in school where they both studied graphic and communication design and illustration at Central Saint Martins London. The duo has been working together on different projects ever since, sharing the same desire and belief that design is a way of living and it should be fun. This is also the vision behind Oh Yeah studio.

OK200
P. 098-099

An Amsterdam-based graphic design studio founded by Mattijs de Wit and Koen Knevel in 2010. They studied together at the Royal Academy of Art in The Hague. The name OK200 is based upon a server response code which means: "your request has succeeded". OK200 is a personal, headstrong, fast, authentic graphic design studio that has experience in working on various projects, from website, magazine to identity.

ONY
P. 061

An agency that integrates high level branding with digital communication skills. ONY designs new experiences of intellectual discovery, deep emotions, powerful insights and overall enjoyment aiming to make the world a more interesting place.

PELLEGRINO, SARA
P. 164-165

Pellegrino was born in 1988.

PENTAGRAM
P. 044-047

The world's largest independent design consultancy leading by design director Paula Scher. Pentagram was founded in 1972 and is run by 19 partners, a group of friends who are all leaders in their individual creative fields. Working from offices in London, New York, San Francisco, Austin and Berlin, the firm specialises in different areas of graphic design, industrial design and architecture, producing printed materials, environments, products and interactive media for a wide range of international clients.

PLANCHENAULT, MORGANE
P. 036-037

A young graphic designer from France. The fresh graduate always try to keep his eyes and mind open for inspiration.

PRIMMER, JOHN
P. 032-033

Currently studying at Falmouth University, Primmer is looking to work internationally to explore his interest of concepts and solutions which have significant positive benefits to society, whilst in turn having fun. He is mad about drawing, cooking, playing guitar and cycling.

PYRAMID STUDIO
P. 222

A multidisciplinary design studio founded by Beatriz Cóias and João Chaves in 2012 with special interest in beautiful images mixed with good ideas, DIY, music and fashion.

ROANDCO
P. 024-025

A multidisciplinary design studio devoted to holistic branding and art direction from print to web. RoAndCo works with a range of small to large companies in the fashion, art, technology and lifestyle industries. Led by award-winning creative director Roanne Adams, the team is committed to working closely with the client to foster a mutually beneficial and collaborative partnership.

ROBSON, THOMAS
P. 148-153

Previously with BBC Television Graphic Design experimenting in creating visually arresting images through the use of defacement art and digital collage techniques, Robson creates new hybrid images which attract attention and repay repeat viewings, whilst in parallel attacking and subverting the cultural carapace of how the source fine art imagery is traditionally read.

ROZENFELDE, MAIJA
P. 028

Started her career working for 4 years as an art director in a full service advertising agency Taivas Ogilvy, Latvia, Rozenfelde later realised her passion for packaging design and moved to the New York City. In 2013, Rozenfelde graduated in Communications and Package Design from Pratt Institute, USA. She is now an independent graphic and packaging designer.

SANS COLOUR
P. 140-141

An independent design studio in Oslo, Norway founded in 2014 by Swedish graphic designer Joakim Jansson with more than 12 years of work experience within graphic and interactive design. Before setting up the studio, Jansson worked for 5 years as a senior designer at the renowned design studio Bleed.

SATO, NOBUHIRO & FRIESEN, HALEY
P. 208-209

"Originally from Shizuoka, Japan and spent 8 years to his own rock band activity in Tokyo, Sato is a creative designer currently based in San Francisco. He studied graphic design at Orange Coast College and has been freelancing graphic and web design since 2011.

Originally from Minnesota, USA, Friesen is a Toronto based photographer specialises in editorial, documentary and dance photography and has spent the last four years at Ryerson University developing her portfolio in these genres. She also works in collaboration with other fine artists to create multimedia bodies of work. These collaborations consist of painting, calligraphy, wax and dance."

SAWDUST
P. 196-197

Since its inception in 2006, Sawdust has been breaking new ground with experimental typography, and clean and clear communication centring around type. Sharing a passion for typography, founders Rob Gonzalez and Jonathan Quainton work with custom typography, image-making, identity and art direction across music, art & culture, fashion, corporate and advertising sectors. The studio's clients include Airside, Leo Burnett, Saatchi, Beautiful/Decay, Creative Review and Novum.

SILLY THING
P. 136-137

Founded by TK in 2000, SILLY THING is one of the most influential multimedia creative agency in Asia, with vast experience in branding, digital and print projects. Well known for its collaborations with many notable international brands, including COMME des GARCONS, Undercover and NIKE, SILLY THING is dedicated to establish a unique aesthetic with an emphasis on visual excellence across the sectors of fashion, lifestyle and design.

SIXSTATION WORKSHOP
P. 176-177, 198

Sixstation dedicates to the art of six senses, and their creative belief is to let the mind flow free between sensibility and consciousness. The workshop shuttles among branding and identity, digital media, publication, illustration, typography and visual art. The beyond-conventions thinking and modern eastern aesthetics soaked in multi-cultural essences, providing the workshop a solid aesthetic quality and creative vision.

SOPA GRAPHICS
P. 121

A little studio with great ideas. To inform and to surprise is what SOPA believes their work is meant to be. They reinvent themselves in every work searching for a touching difference, where they find their value at.

SPIROS HALARIS STUDIO
P. 124-125, 172-175

The multidisciplinary illustrator, designer and art director has been commissioned to create work for various of international brands, publications and companies such as Harrods, Printemps, Bloomingdale's, ELLE, Walt Disney, Sephora, Design Museum, The Mayfair Hotel, Tom Ford, D&G, Topshop. His work has been exhibited in London, Paris, New York, Brussels and also at the Arnhem Mode Biennale.

SPREAD STUDIO
P. 042-043

A multidisciplinary design studio specialised in the fashion and lifestyle industry. The studio works cross disciplinary through creative direction, brand design and collaborations in a mix of creativity and commerce.

STAHL R
P. 132-133

Berlin based design studio founded in 2012 by Tobias Röttger and Susanne Stahl. Both research and concept driven, Stahl R creates unique design solutions for a broad range of clients from the commercial and the cultural fields. Their services include visual identities, publication design, environmental design, editorial and art direction, to time-based media and digital projects. The studio has been rewarded with national and international awards for its thoughtful, intelligent and innovative work.

STUDIO BAND
P. 129

A graphic design consultancy based in Adelaide, Australia specialising in the creation and development of dynamic and unique graphic solutions that engage and connect with their audience. By working closely with clients, Band is able to deliver thoughtful, intelligent and strategic solutions that maintain a high level of execution and integrity.

STUDIO BRAVE
P. 102-103

Founded in 2002, Brave is a design studio driven by the creation of unique, distinctive and memorable brand communication. With the guiding vision comes from its name, brave thinking leads to unexpected outcomes which engage the audience and build emotional connections with the brand. Through research and discovery they develop a deep understanding of clients' business in order to define objectives, unlock potential and differentiate.

STUDIO FNT
P. 122

Founded in 2006 and based in Seoul, Korea, studio fnt focuses on prints, identities, interactive and digital media, typeface design, media art collaborations and more. In 2010, the design studio launched fnt press, a publisher of books and other materials regarding design, art and anything inventive.

STUDIO HAUSHERR
P. 085

A small graphic design agency based in Berlin, Studio Hausherr focuses on corporate, editorial and web design for clients in the field of art, fashion and culture, providing a comprehensive design and visual communication tailored to suit their needs.

TADA, YUJIRO
P. 186-187

A Tokyo based artist and photographer with his work demonstrated on Behance.

TARDY, JULES
P. 078

First in London, UK and now in Brooklyn, USA, the multidisciplinary graphic designer and art director is specialised in design for contemporary culture. After earning the master degree in visual arts, Tardy has since been busy working full time at Mother Design, a sub group of the advertising agency Mother. His projects include a wide range clientele, from independent art galleries to industry leaders such as Google, Microsoft, 1 Hotel and Conde Nast.

THE SOUVENIR SOCIETY
P. 016-017

A collaboration between packaging designer Kasia Gadecki and book designer Allison Colpoys with a shared love for pattern, illustration, packaging and design. Based in Melbourne, Australia, the duo only uses FSC certified, 100% recycled paper stock, and bio-degradable, compostable cello packaging. Their stationery range includes cards, tags, twine, wrapping paper and reusable wrapping cloth.

THERE IS
P. 084

Founded by Sean Freeman, the studio is specialised in creative typography, illustration and art direction. Based in East London, Freeman creates award winning typographic treatments and illustrations for a varied range of clients globally from advertising to music, editorial and publishing. Known to be powerful with a dynamic and organic fusion between elements, his work is featured in numerous books and international magazines.

THISISLOVE DESIGN STUDIO
P. 100-101

From graphic design to web or experimental media projects and focused on art direction, communication design, new media solutions and interactivity, one of the main objectives for thisislove™ design studio is to create a multidisciplinary platform. The studio establishd a cool normality and its projects pretend to questionning the process of creation and interaction between people, objects and signs. They make ideas real, with a great eye for detail and hidden meanings, without intending any particular sense of style.

TOM HINGSTON STUDIO
P. 142-143

"The studio of the established creative director and graphic designer who is renowned for his innovative and highly thoughtful approach to art direction and design spanning print, digital, moving image and experiential. The winner of numerous awards, particularly for its work in music, has been collaborated extensively with some of the world's most well-known artists, including Grace Jones, Nick Cave, The Chemical Brothers, The Rolling Stones, Lady Gaga, Robbie Williams and Massive Attack.

Following his early acclaim in music, Hingston has subsequently been appointed as Art Director for numerous fashion brands including Christian Dior, Alexander McQueen and Lancôme. Further campaigns and collaborations in fashion have included work with Nike, Harvey Nichols, Mappin & Webb, Dior Parfums, Levis and jewellery designer Solange Azagury-Partridge.

A natural shift into moving image, over the last five years, has led to a number of film title collaborations with directors including Joe Wright; Pride & Prejudice, Atonement and Anna Karenina and Anton Corbijn for Control. Hingston's most recent collaboration is with David Bowie on the video for 'I'd Rather Be High', taken from his 2013 album 'The Next Day'. "

TRIBORO
P. 194

The Brooklyn based design duo of David Heasty and Stefanie Weigler. Natives of Texas and Germany, Heasty and Weigler attract a global client base ranging from innovative start-ups to respected international brands. Triboro creates design solutions for clients in publishing, art, fashion, music, lifestyle, and for cultural institutions. Its partners have won numerous industry awards and their work has been featured in publications and exhibitions around the world.

TSTO
P. 054-055, 123

A Helsinki-based graphic design agency focusing on visual concepts and art direction. Tsto was founded by Johannes Ekholm, Jonatan Eriksson, Inka Järvinen, Matti Kunttu, Jaakko Pietiläinen and Antti Uotila.

TWEE
P. 058-059

Meaning in Dutch for "the two", De Twee consists of two independent graphic designers who are brothers and best friends residing in Antwerp, Belgium. The duo is specialised in corporate identity and branding with a fond interest in print.

TYMOTE
P. 138-139

A graphic design bureau of a group of young creatives in their 20s based in Tokyo. Centering around graphic design, the team also works on moving image, computer graphics, music, interface design, web design, etc.

UNELEFANTE
P. 020-021

An original and exciting destination where the ordinary is transformed into extraordinary experiences, UNELEFANTE designs, produces and curates collections of unique and inspiring gifts, all handcrafted in México.

WANG ZHI-HONG STUDIO
P. 215

Born in 1975 in Taipei, Wang started his studio in 2000. In 2008 and 2012, he collaborated with trade publishers launching "INSIGHT" and "SOURCE" respectively, featuring translated titles on art and design. A six-time winner of Golden Butterfly Awards, Taiwan's highest honor for excellence in book design, the designer has received many international awards and recognitions, including Kaoru Kasai's Choice Award and Silver Awards from HKDA Global Design Awards, as well as Excellent Works from Tokyo Type Directors Club Annual Awards.

WESTERMANN, SARA
P. 210-211, 223

Sspecialised in poster, editorial design, illustration, photography and art direction, the portuguese multidisciplinary graphic designer works mainly in artistic and cultural mediums. Graduated from ESAD – School of Art & Design and previously worked under Stefan Sagmeister and ExperimentaDesign Biennale, Westermann is currently working at Casa da Música, a Concert Hall in Porto.

YOUNG, AUSTIN
P. 018-019

The pop-culture architect, photographer and trans media artist has been documenting pop, celebrity, sub, and trans culture since 1985 through portraiture. Young's video works play with pop-culture and camp, celebrity, gender and identity. His photographs have been featured in major publications such as Interview Magazine, OK, and Flaunt and have been in solo exhibitions and projects at LACMA in Los Angeles, Berkeley Art Museum in Berkeley and as well as groups shows at Los Angeles Contemporary Exhibitions Stephen Cohen Gallery in Los Angeles. In addition to photography and filmmaking, Young is the co-founder of Fallen Fruit, an art collective who use fruit as a common denominator to change the way you think about the world.

MAKING A SPLASH:
GRAPHICS THAT FLOW

First published and distributed by
viction workshop ltd

viction:ary

viction workshop ltd
Unit C, 7/F, Seabright Plaza, 9-23 Shell Street,
North Point, Hong Kong
Url: www.victionary.com   Email: we@victionary.com
 www.facebook.com/victionworkshop
 www.twitter.com/victionary_
 www.weibo.com/victionary

Edited and produced by viction:ary

Concepts & art direction by Victor Cheung
Book design by viction workshop ltd
Cover Image: A Lady With Red Ground by Thomas Robson

©2014 viction workshop ltd
Copyright on text and design work is held by respective designers and
contributors.

All rights reserved. No part of this publication may be reproduced,
stored in retrieval systems or transmitted in any form or by any means,
electronic, mechanical, photocopying, recording or any information
storage, without written permissions from respective copyright owner(s).

All artwork and textual information in this book are based on the
materials offered by designers whose work has been included. While
every effort has been made to ensure their accuracy, viction:workshop
does not accept any responsibility, under any circumstances, for any
errors or omissions.

ISBN 978-988-12228-6-2
Printed and bound in China

ACKNOWLEDGEMENTS

We would like to thank all the designers and companies who have
involved in the production of this book. This project would not have been
accomplished without their significant contribution to the compilation of
this book. We would also like to express our gratitude to all the producers for
their invaluable opinions and assistance throughout this entire project. The
successful completion also owes a great deal to many professionals in the
creative industry who have given us precious insights and comments. And to
the many others whose names are not credited but have made specific input
in this book, we thank you for your continuous support the whole time.

FUTURE EDITIONS

If you wish to participate in viction:ary's future projects and publications,
please send your website or portfolio to submit@victionary.com